One year in America

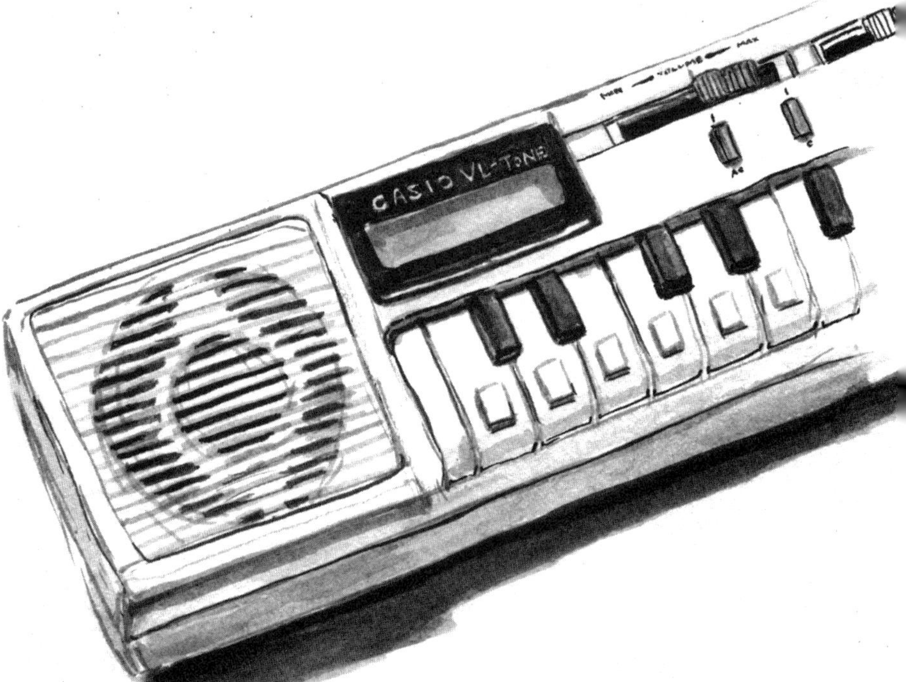
CASIO VL-TONE

Library and Archives Canada Cataloguing in Publication

Belliveau, Elisabeth, 1979-, author, illustrator
One year in America / Elisabeth Belliveau.

ISBN 978-1-894994-87-3 (pbk.)

1. Graphic novels. I. Title.

PN6734.O528B44 2014   741.5'971   C2014-905151-4

Printed and bound by Gauvin Press in Quebec, Canada
First Edition

Conundrum Press
Greenwich, NS
www.conundrumpress.com

Conundrum Press acknowledges the financial support of the
Canada Council for the Arts and the Government of Canada
through the Canada Book Fund toward its publishing activities.

Canada Council   Conseil des Arts
for the Arts   du Canada

Canada

One year in America

elisabeth belliveau

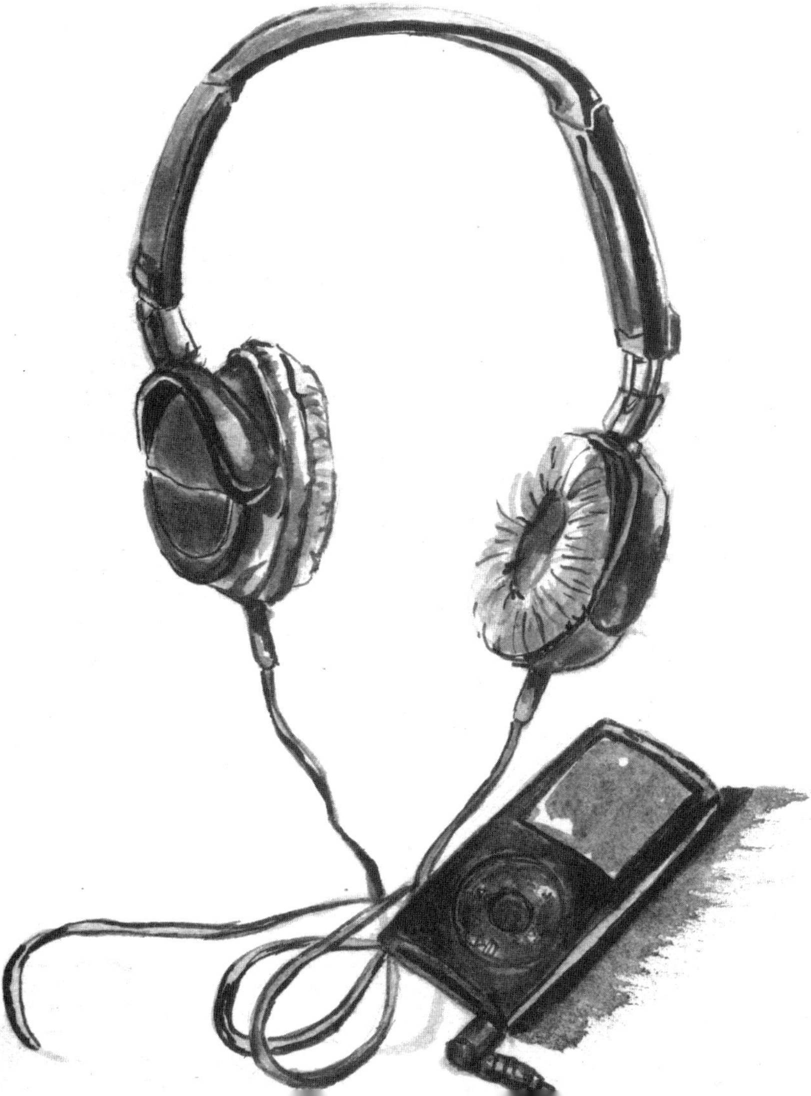

Balance

The most important psychological as well as
Physical influence in human perception is mans
need for balance, to have his two feet planted
firmly on the ground and to know if he is to remain
upright in any circumstance, in any attitude,
with some reasonable certainty.

Donis A. Donis
A Primer of Visual Literacy
MIT Press 1973

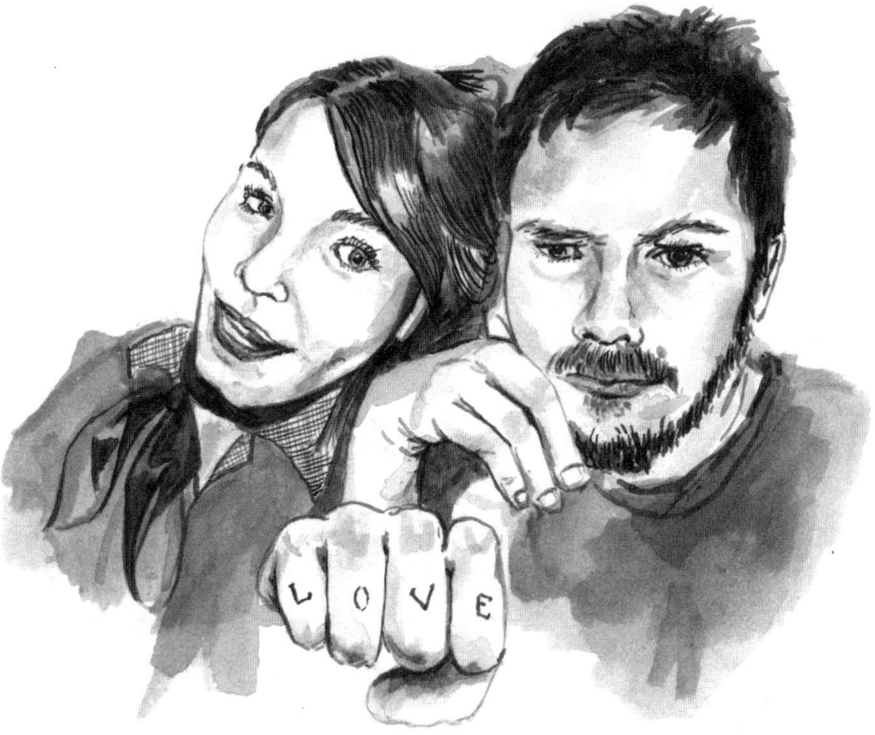
LOVE

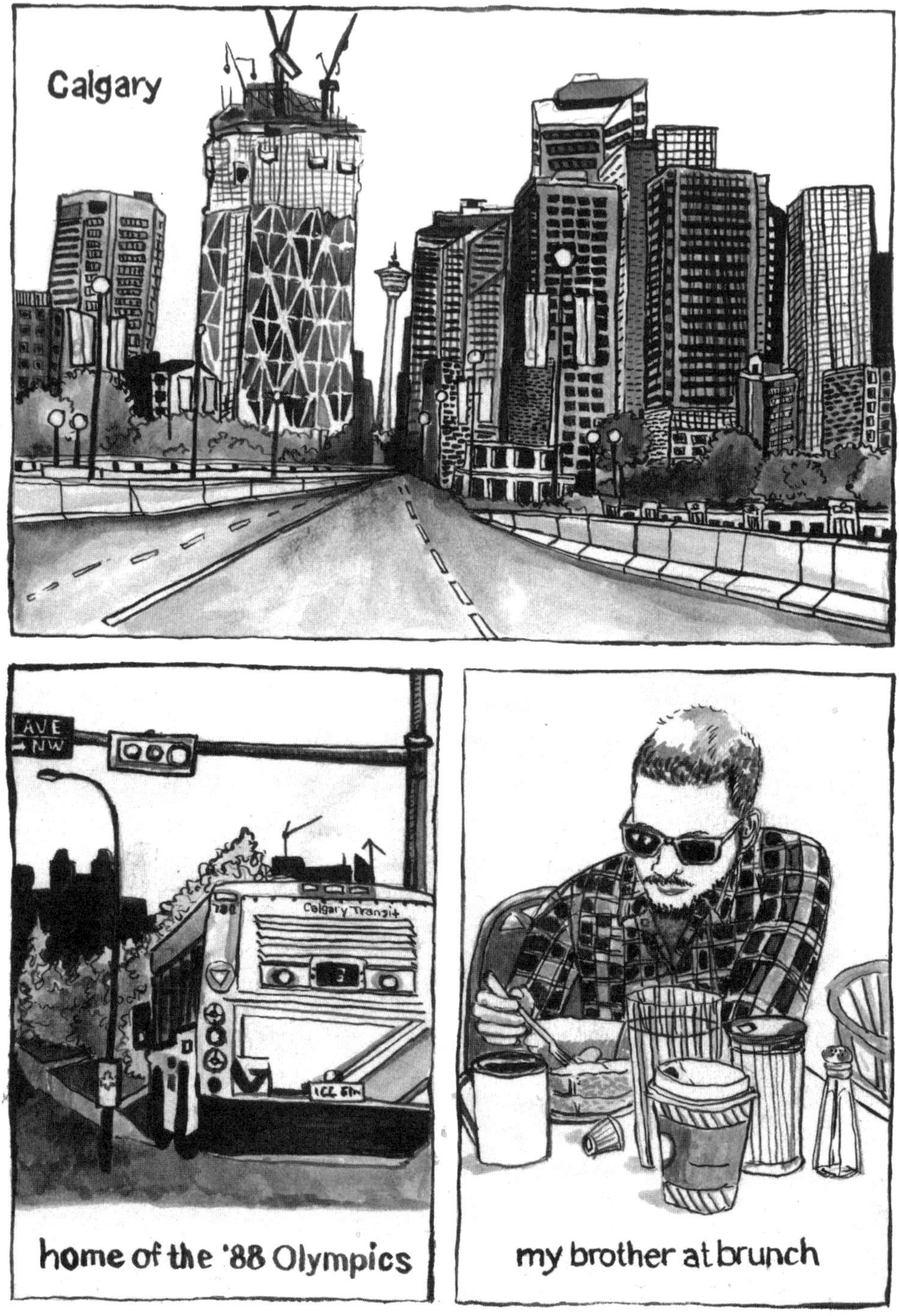
Calgary
AVE
NW
Calgary Transit
home of the '88 Olympics
my brother at brunch

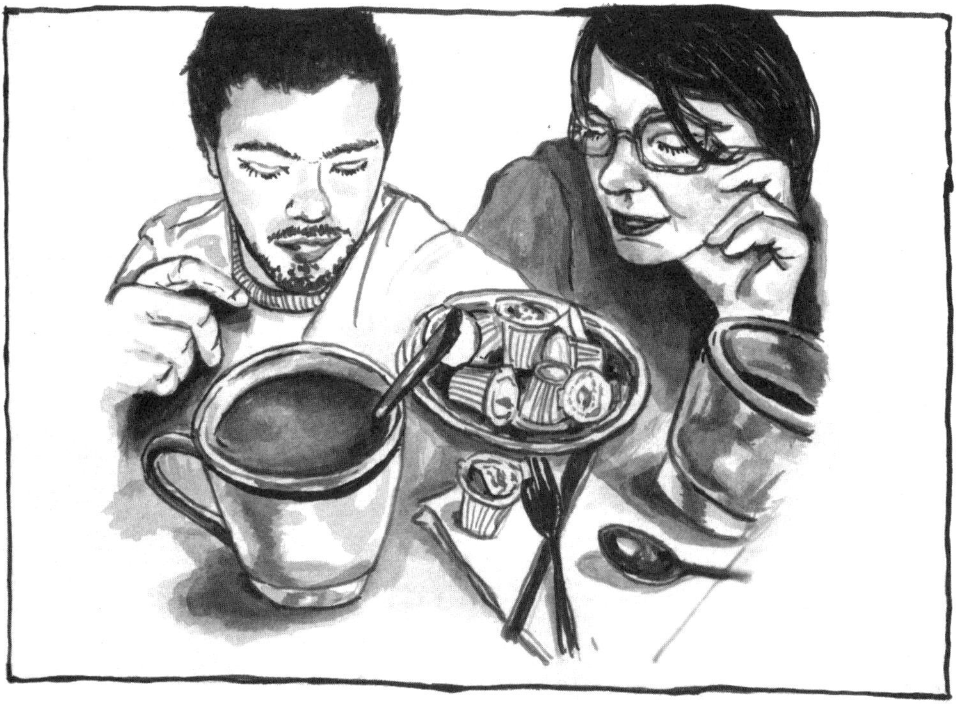

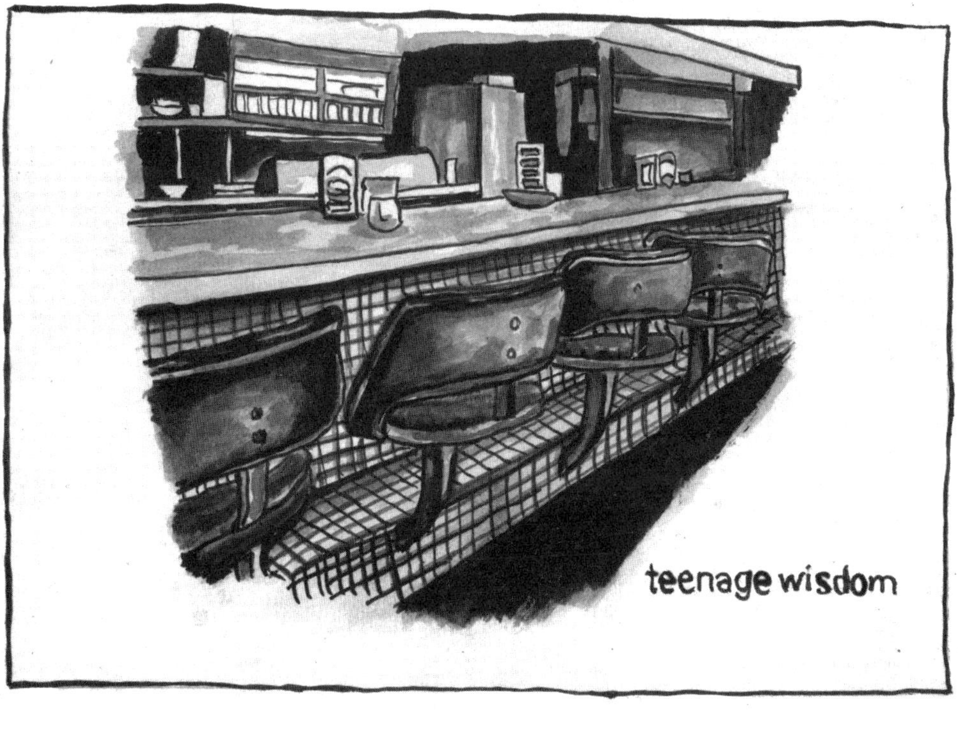
teenage wisdom

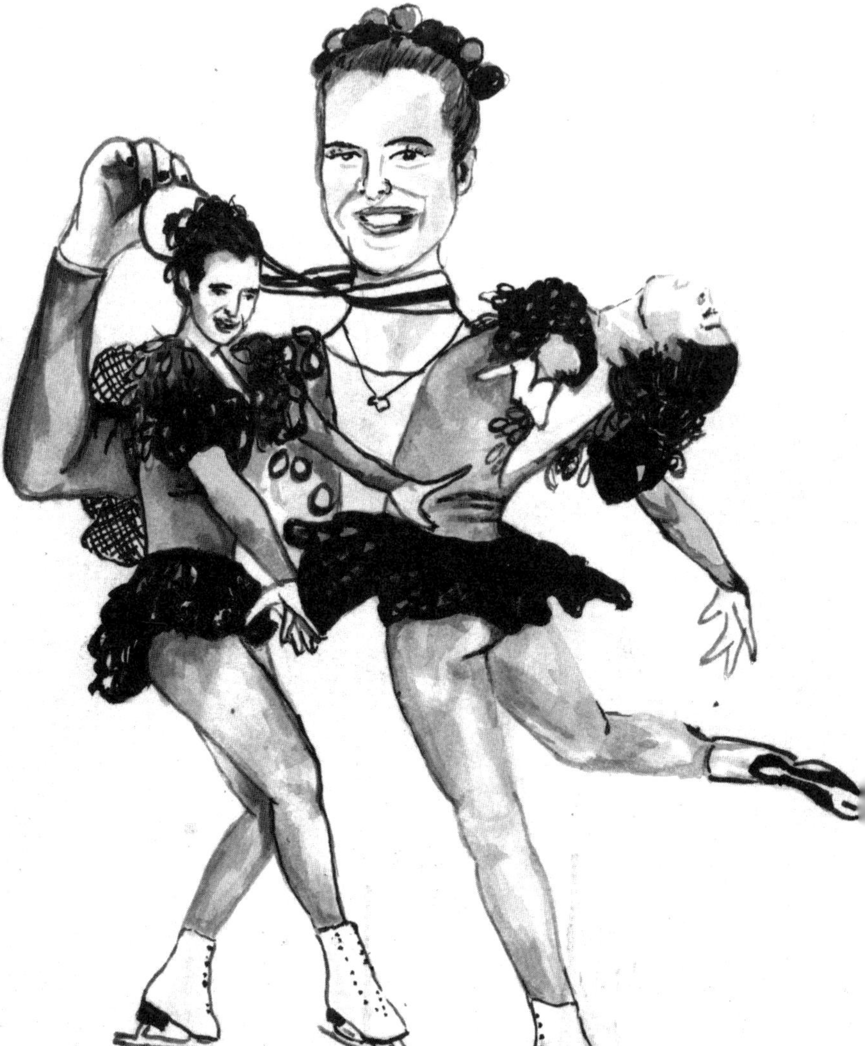

Katarina Witt was
my figure skating hero.
but then she got super
naked.

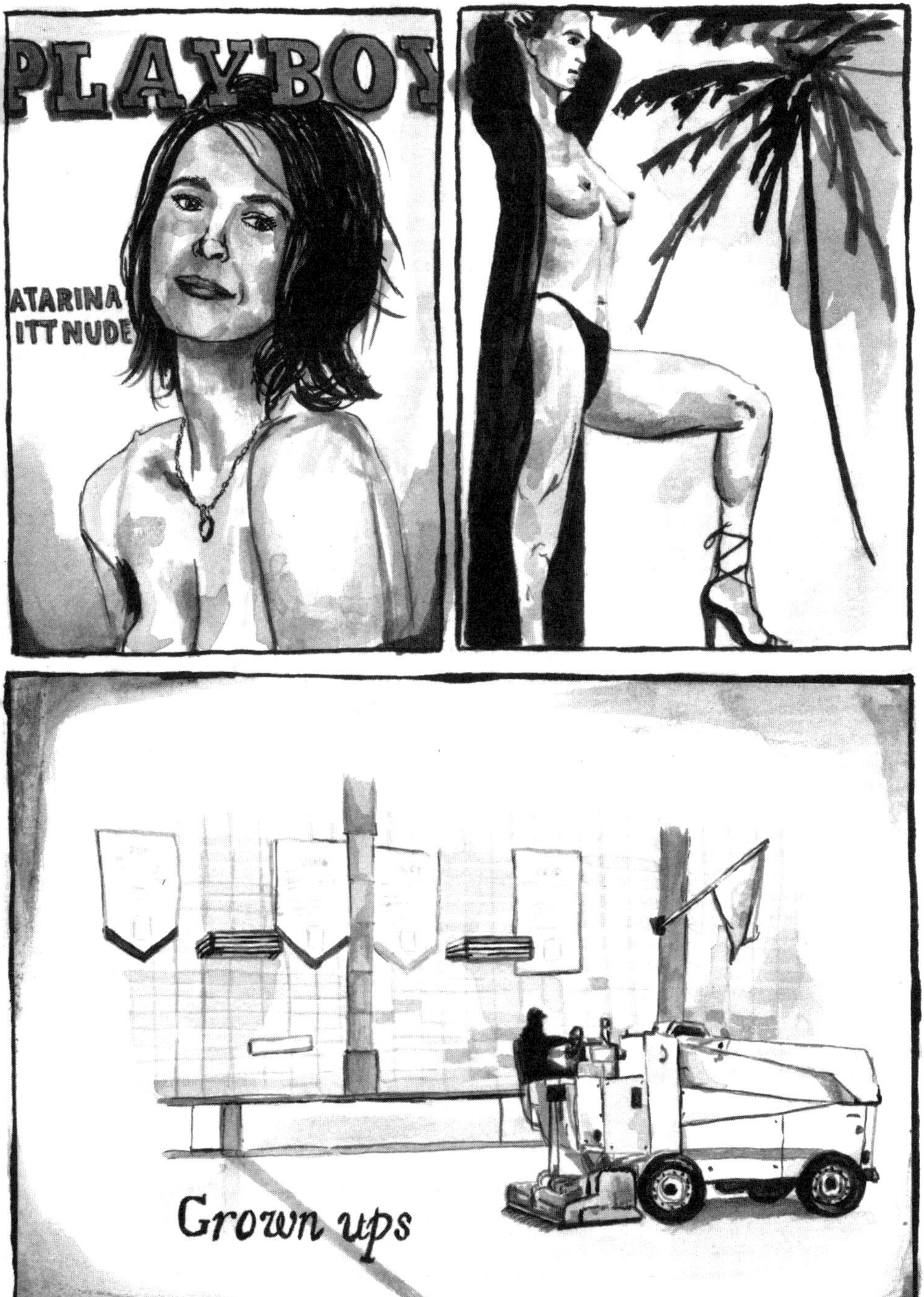
PLAYBOY
ATARINA
ITT NUDE
Grown ups

More careful heroes closer to home -

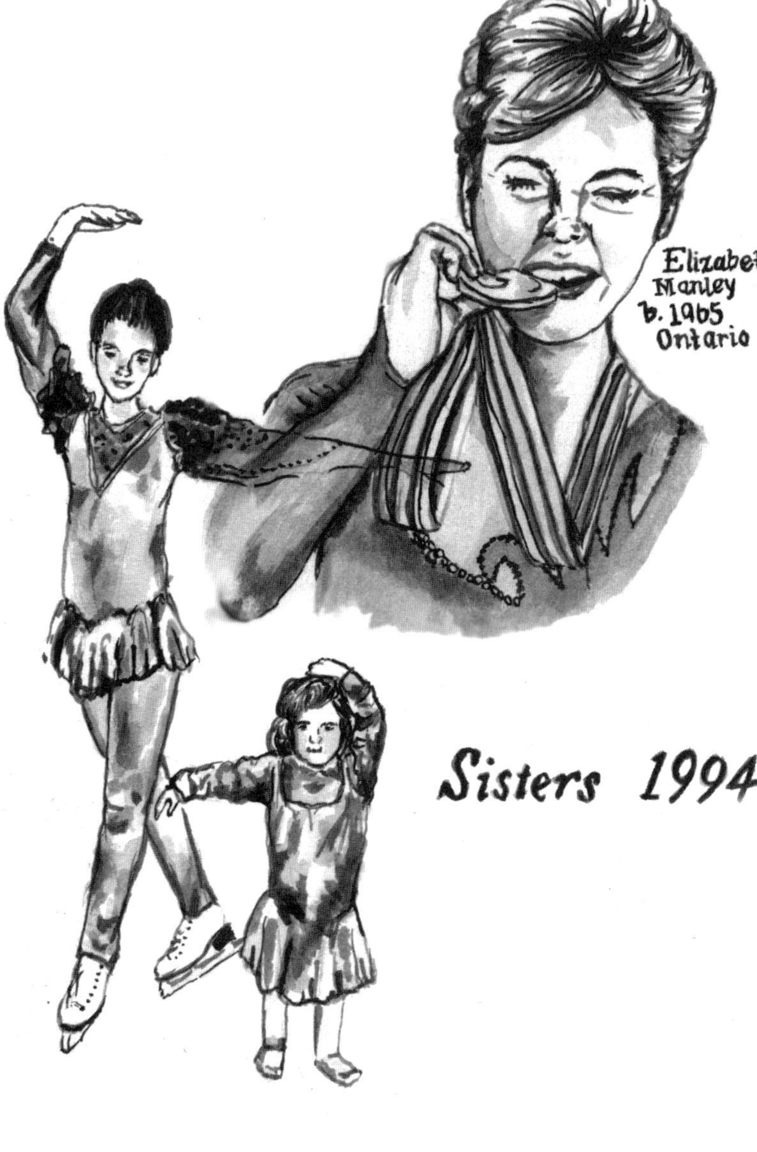
Elizabeth
Manley
b. 1965
Ontario

Sisters 1994

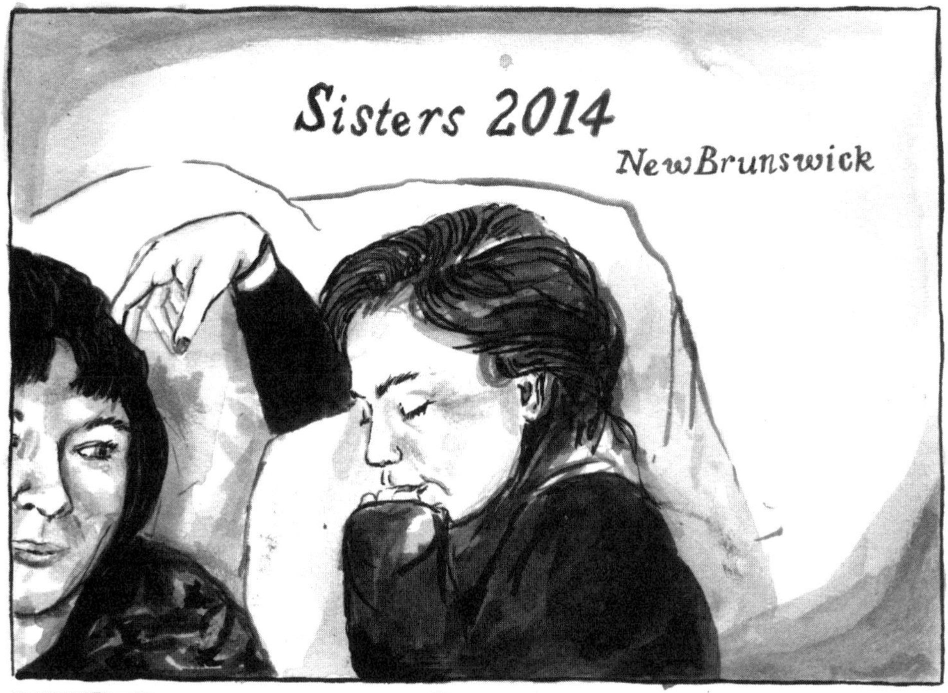
Sisters 2014
NewBrunswick

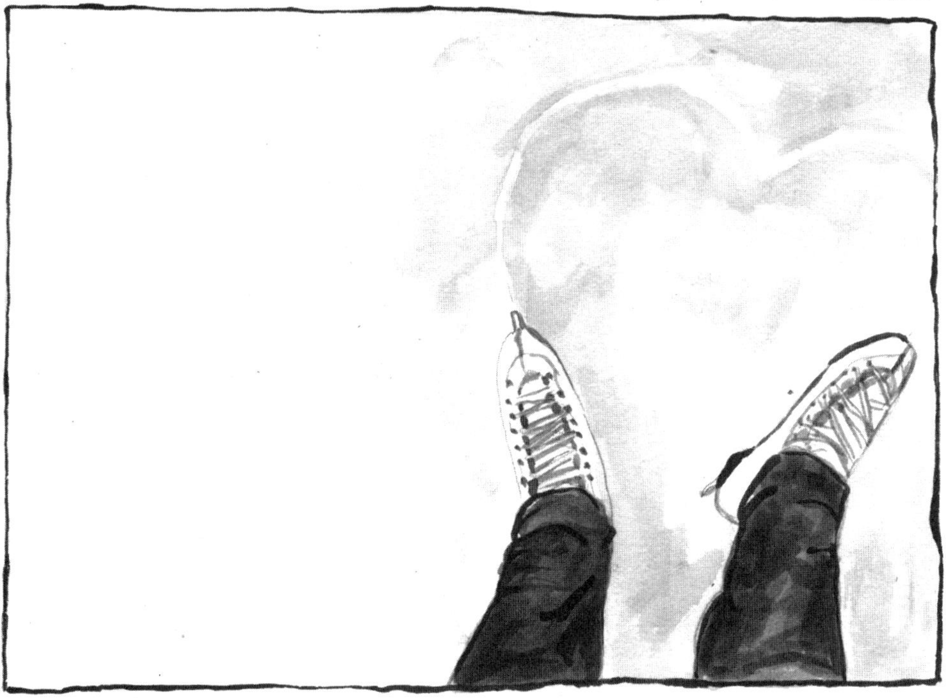

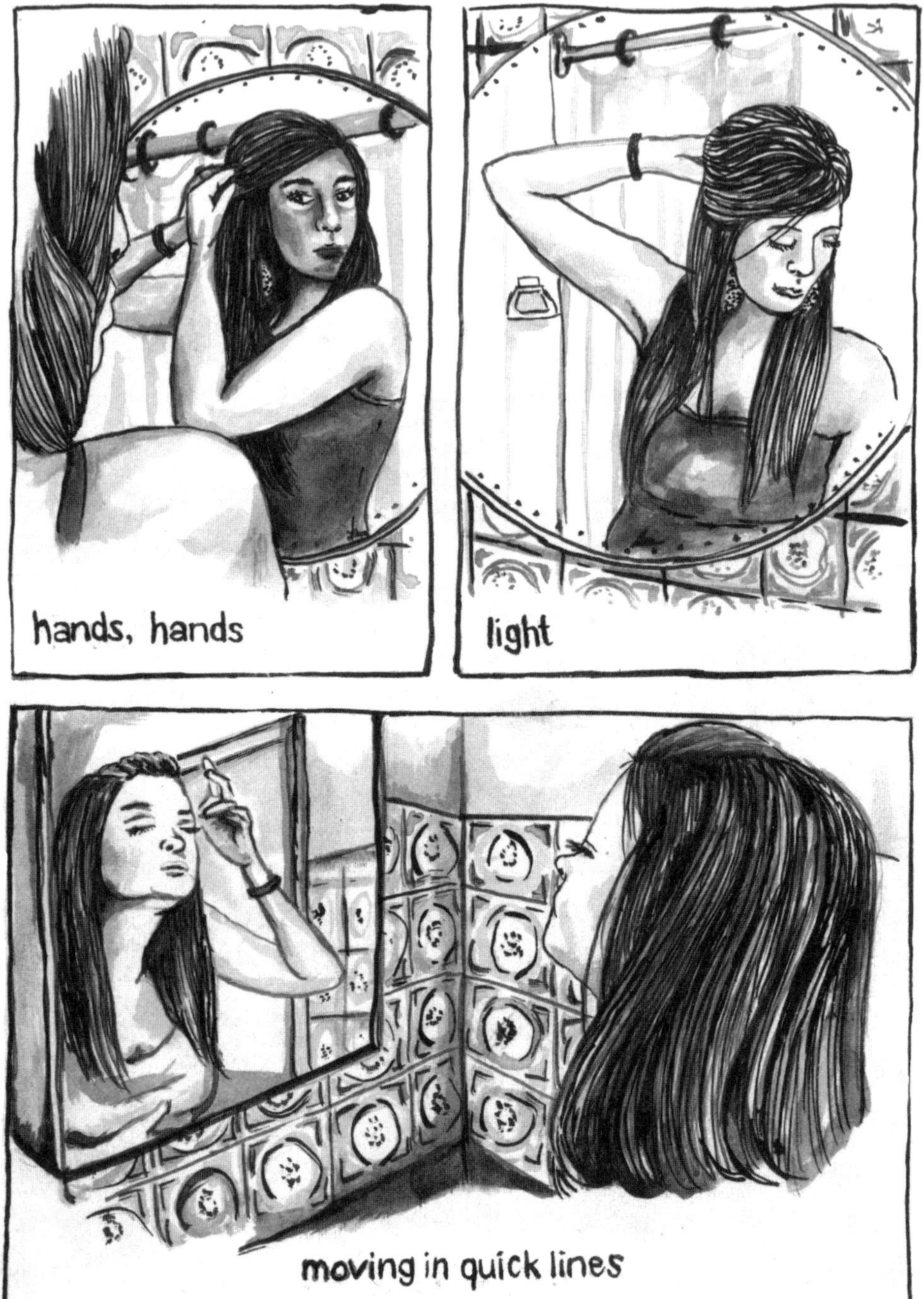
hands, hands
light
moving in quick lines

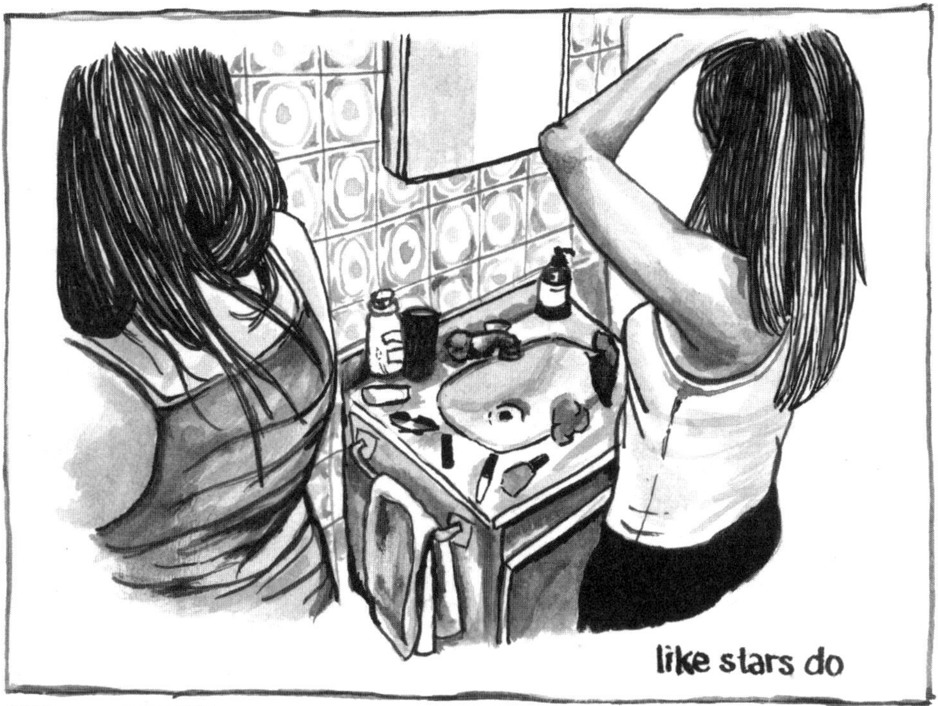
like stars do

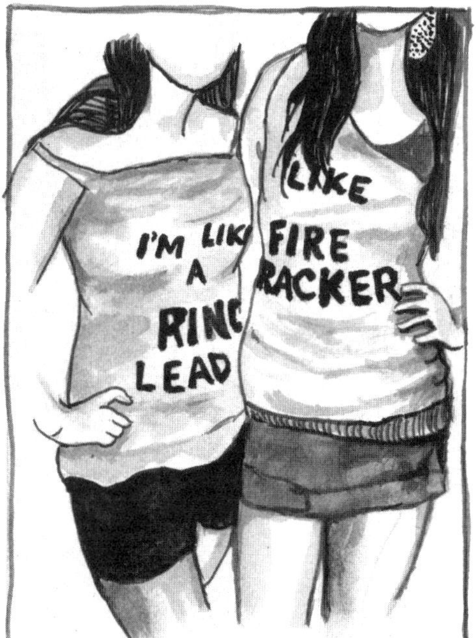
I'M LIK
A
RINC
LEAD
LIKE
FIRE
RACKER

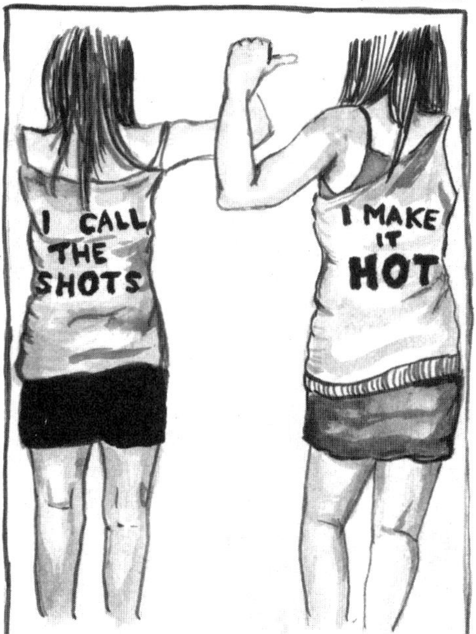
I CALL
THE
SHOTS
I MAKE
IT
HOT

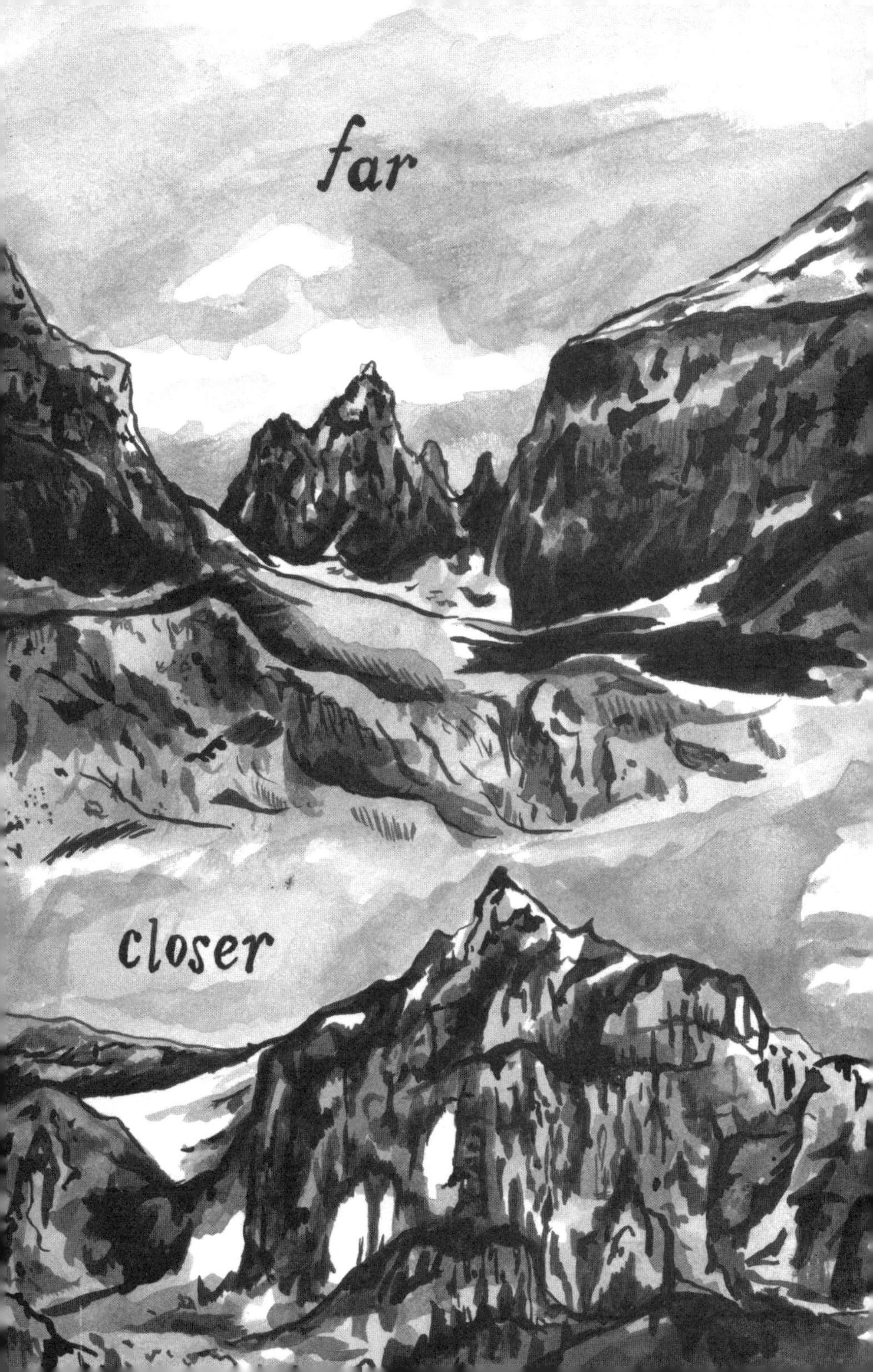
far
closer

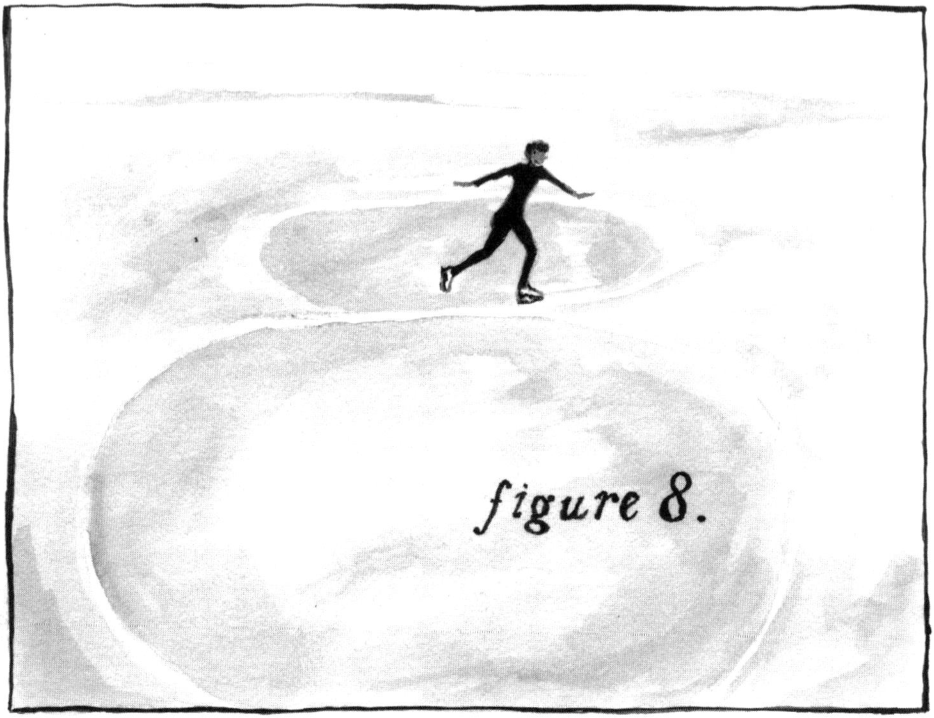
figure 8.

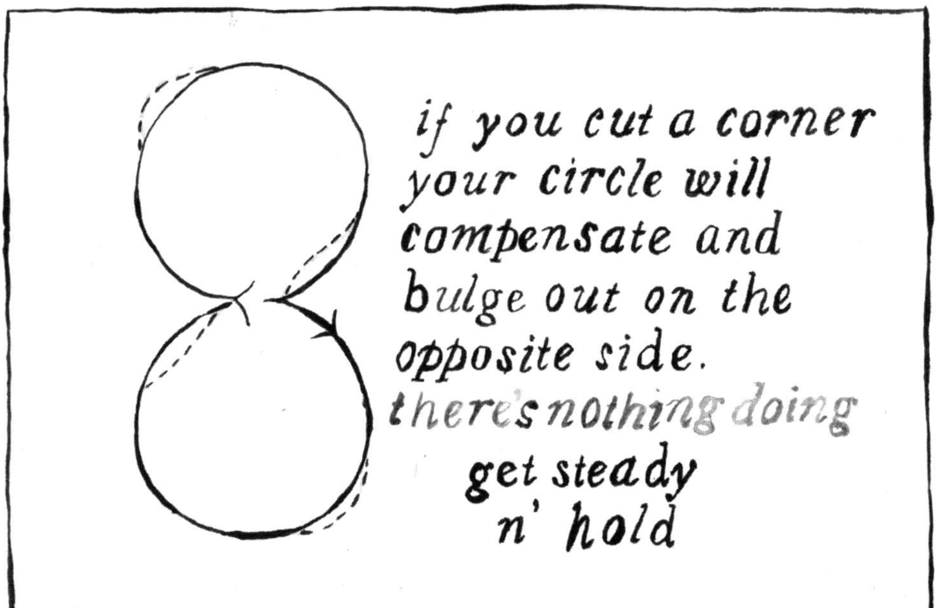
if you cut a corner
your circle will
compensate and
bulge out on the
opposite side.
there's nothing doing
get steady
n' hold

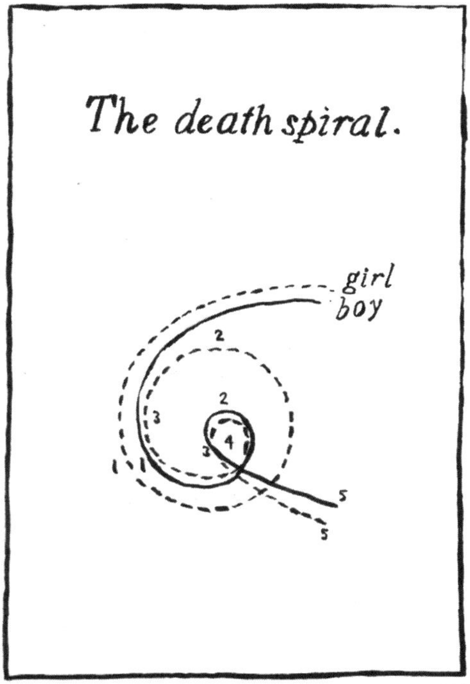
The death spiral.
girl
boy
2
2
3
4
3
1
1
5
5

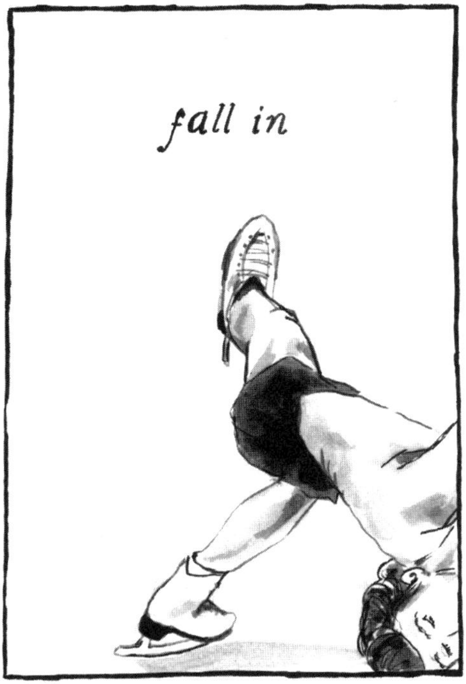
fall in

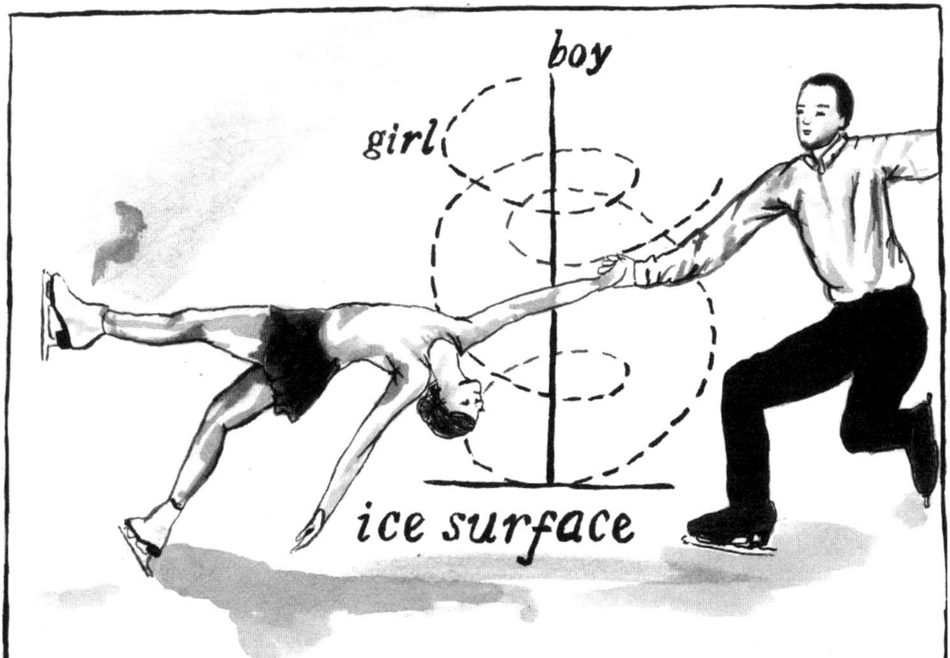
boy
girl
ice surface

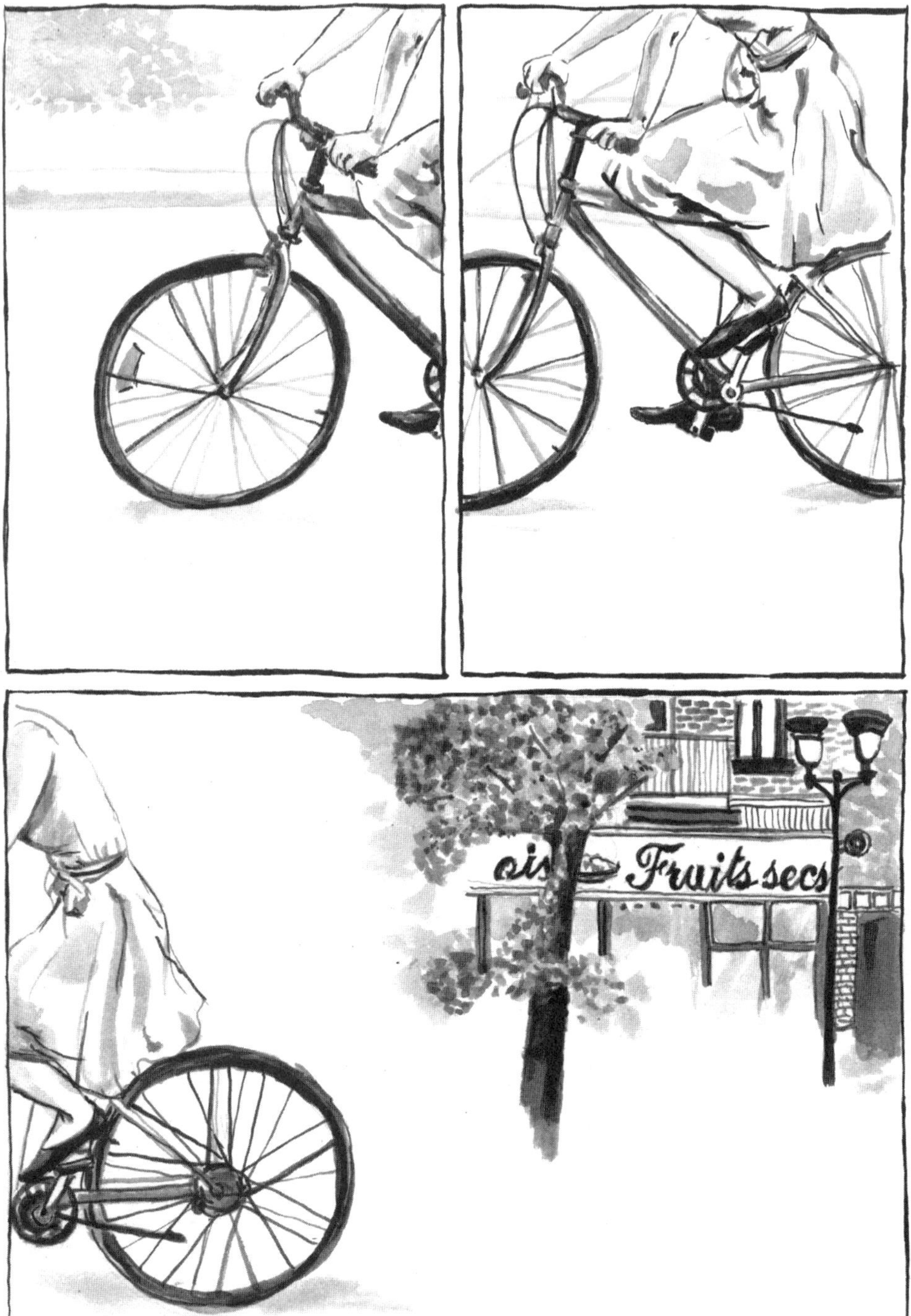
ois Fruits secs

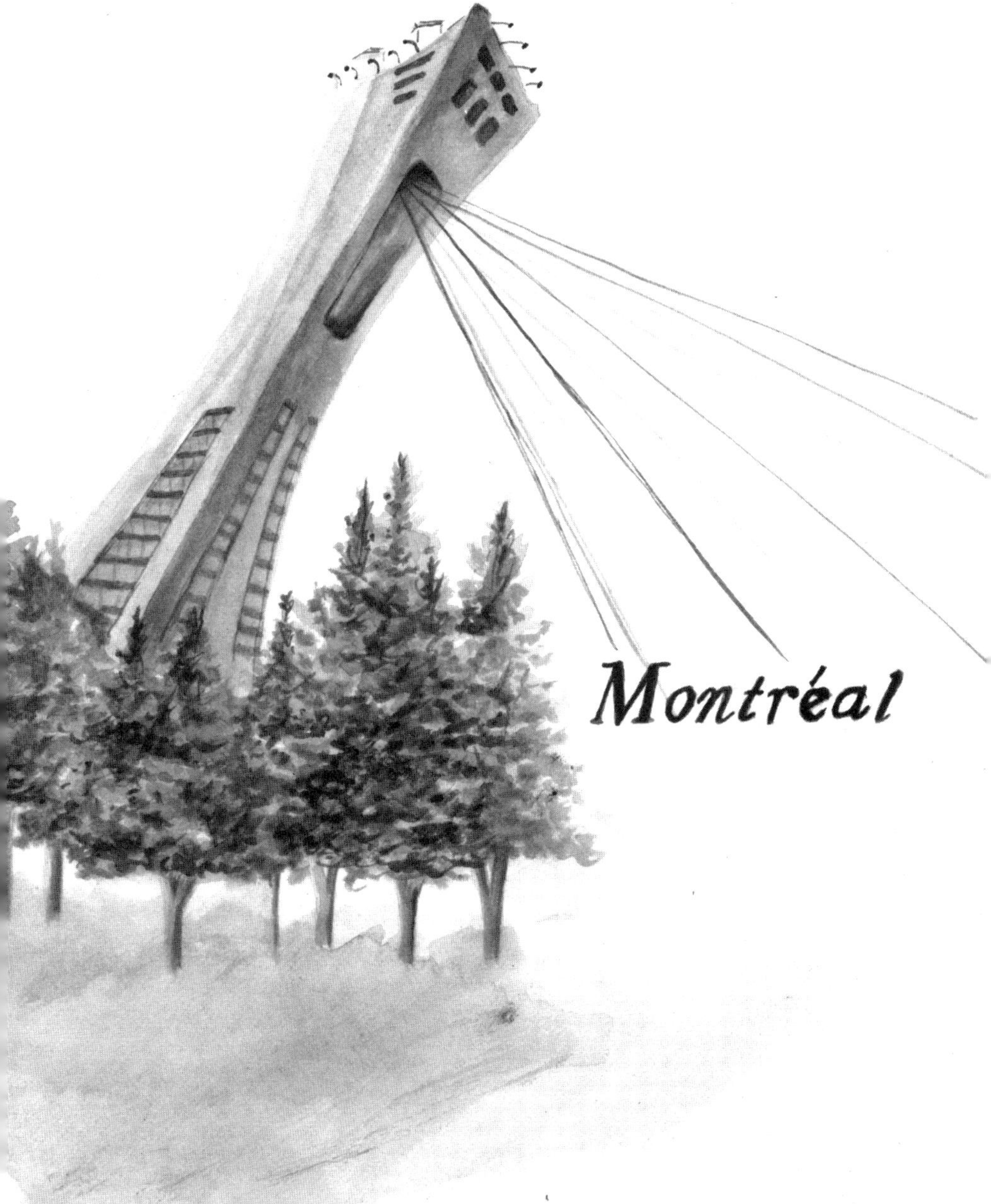

Montréal

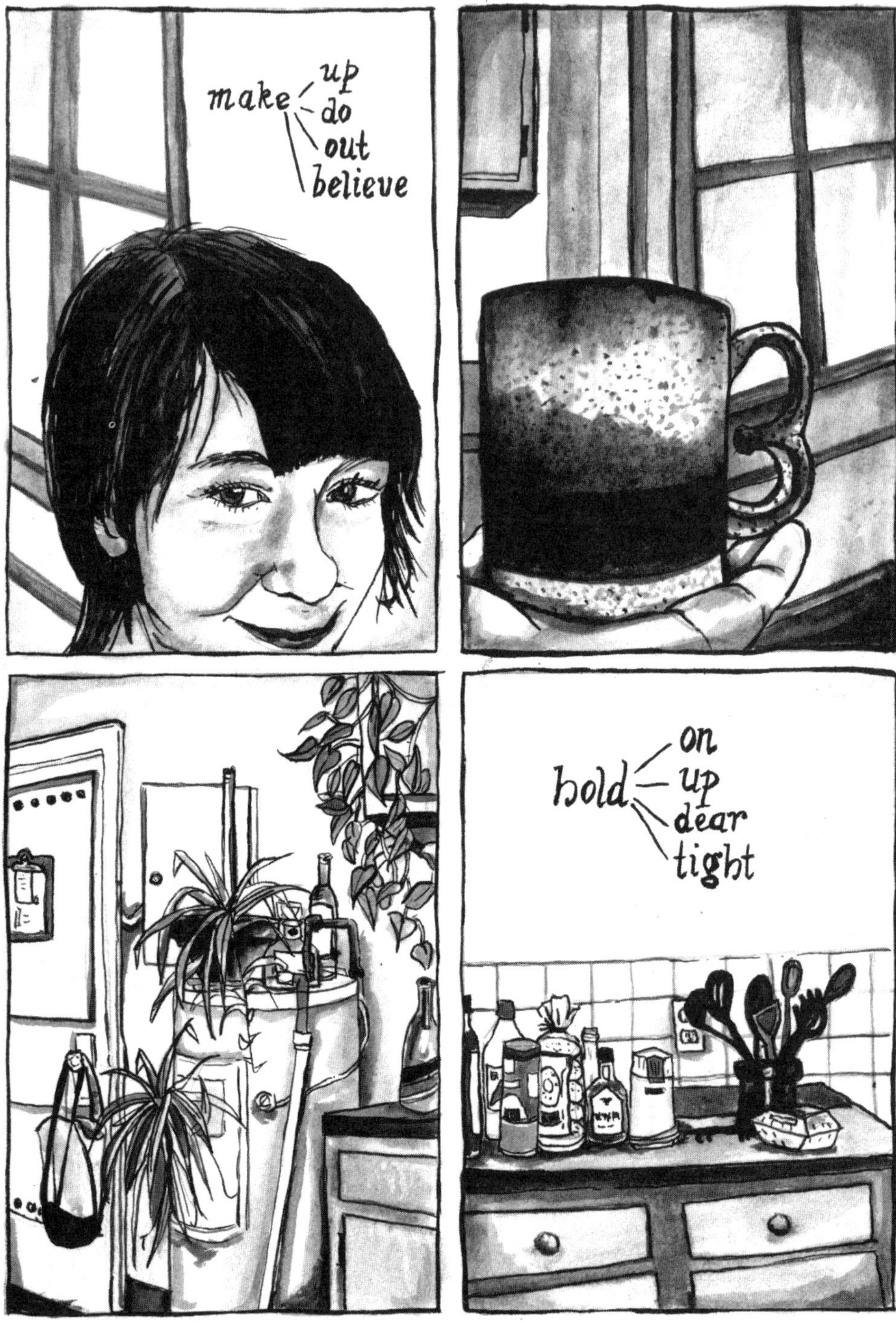
make up
do
out
believe
hold on
up
dear
tight

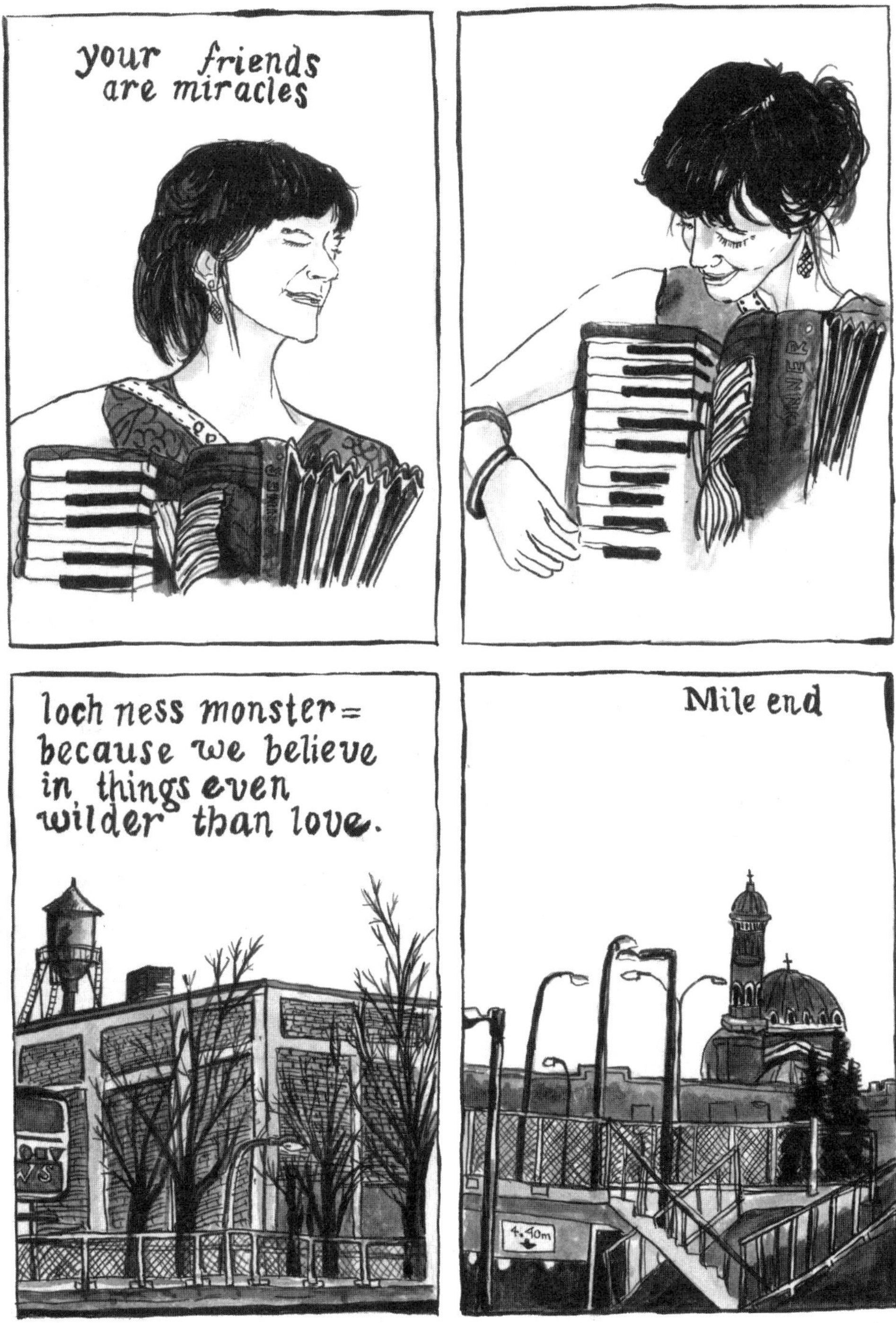
your friends are miracles
loch ness monster= because we believe in things even wilder than love.
Mile end
4.40m

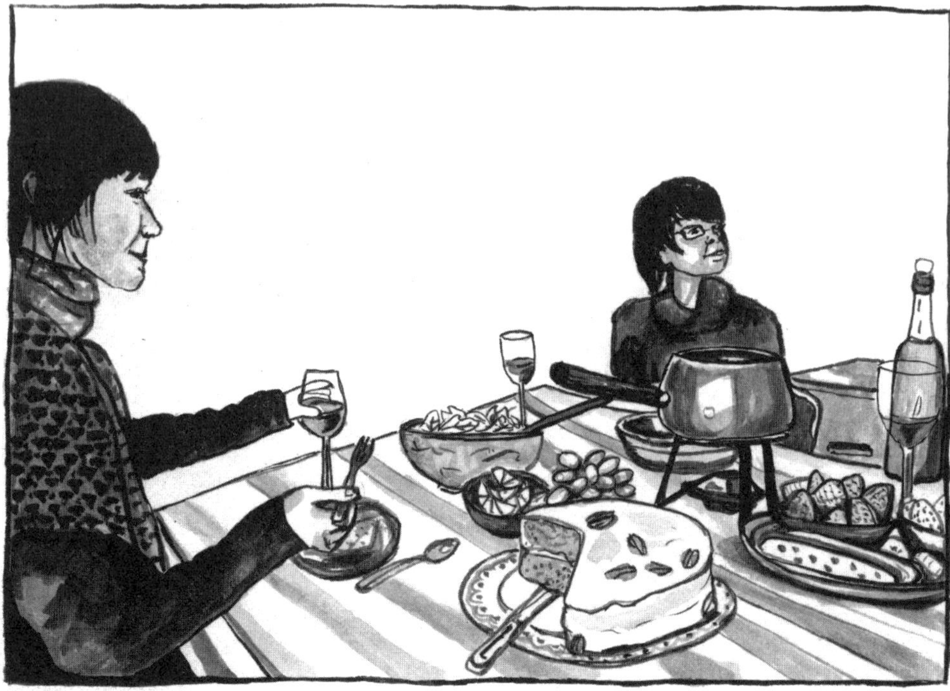

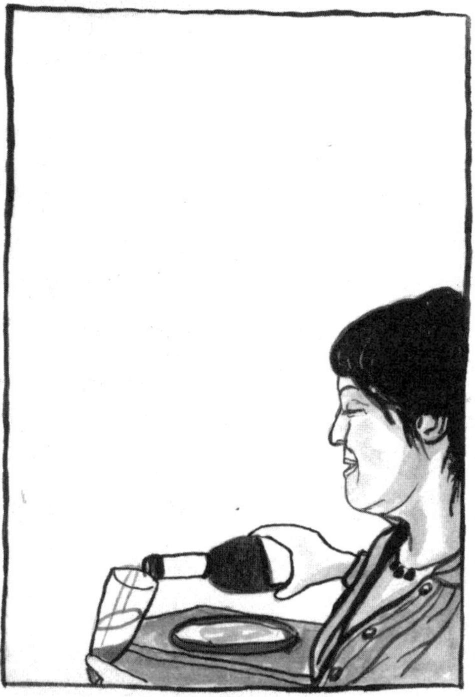

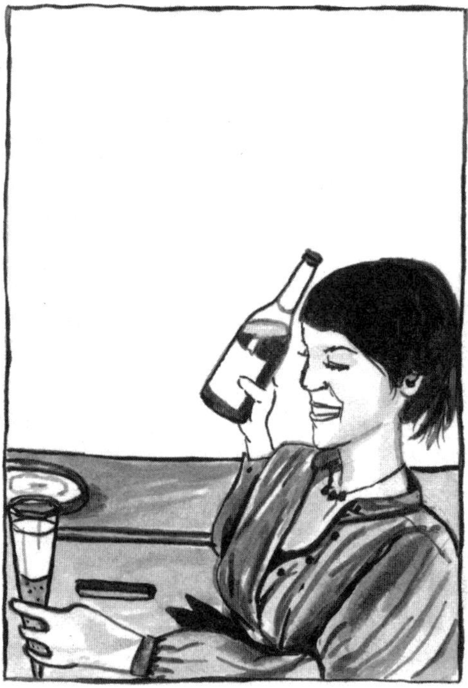

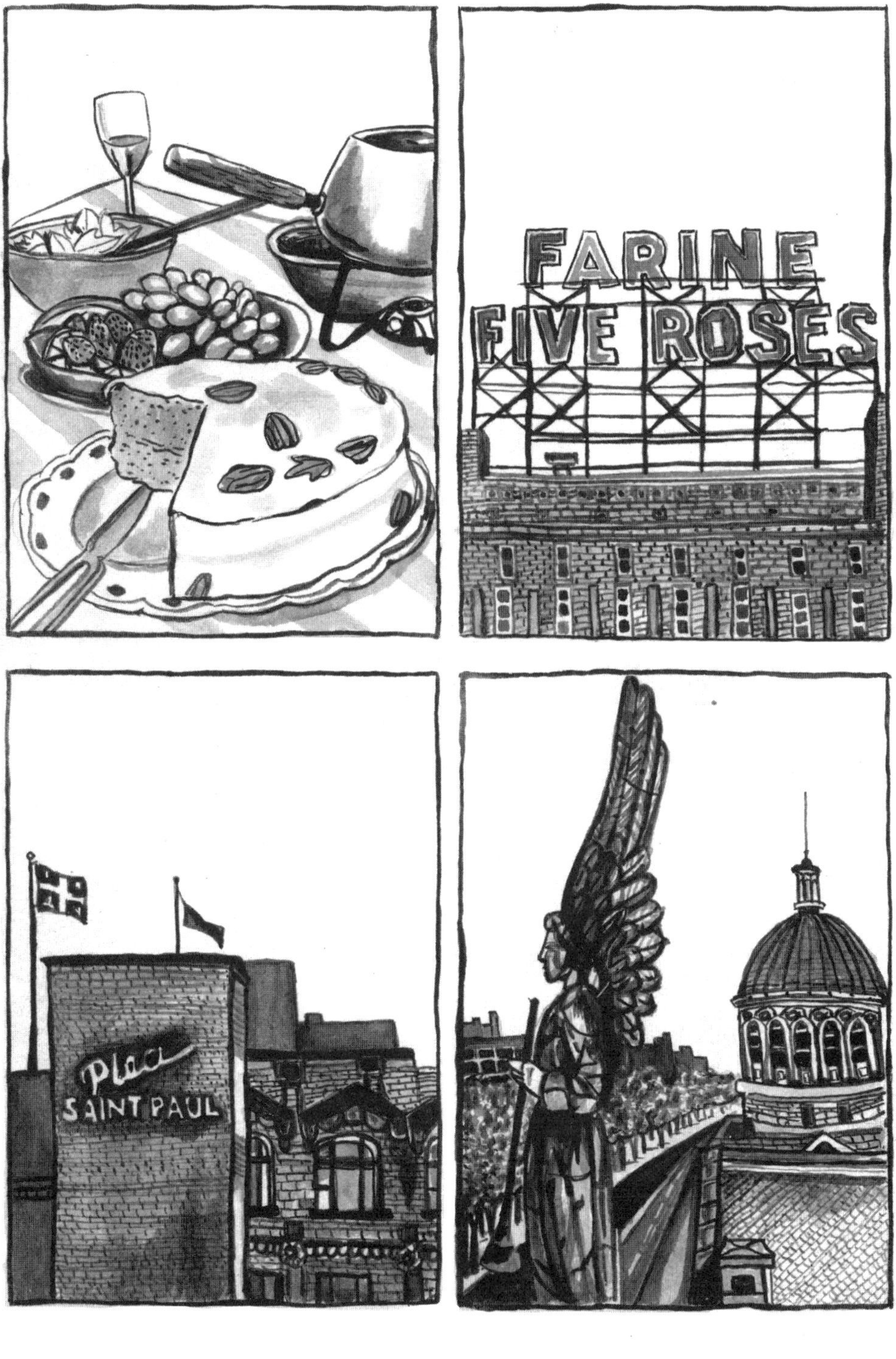
FARINE
FIVE ROSES
SAINT PAUL

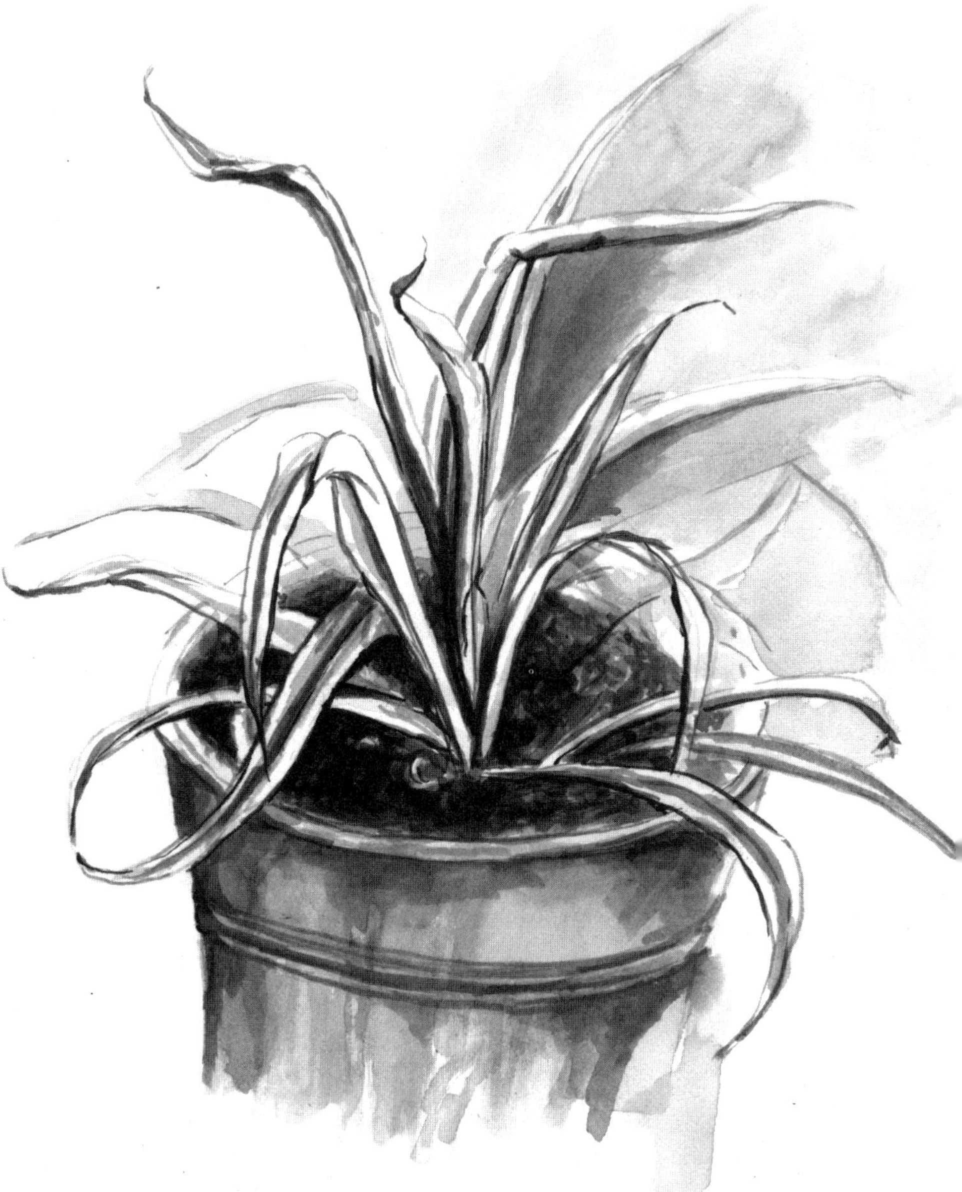

▼

G:
 i got plants today
 think I'll get into houseplants
 how are yours??
 me: they are doing about 80%
2:47 PM two died i threw them out.
 i feel like i gotta move soon –
 G :-(
 me: so maybe houseplants are gonna have to be let go.
 adopted out.
 ?
G: like - out of the apartment?
 me: its too much space and rent for me alone.
 G: :-(
 me: and i think i gotta leave mtl
 G: yes - i understand
 me: it is too hard.
2:48 PM i think maybe in three months?
G: poop
 me: i know it sucks
G: like april?
 me: yeah end of april.
 G: where to??
2:49 PM me: i can't figure out what to do yet ? maybe berlin maybe
calgary?
 if A_____ magically asks me - then _____ ?
 G: oh boy
 me: i am so confused.
the money will run out and i gotta have a plan ...
2:50 PM G: who knew we'd end up finished grad school with nothing
 me: yeah !
 so funny.
G: yeay mfa
 me: no boyfriend no wedding no babies no jobs.
 C O O L =
G: horrors
 me: yeah its the bottoms.
 so things can only improve!
2:51 PM G: 100% potential

i have been up most of the night, in a total panic.
i don't know what my deal is right now - i'm super anxious
and feel like every decision i make is the wrong one. sorry if
this is dramatic - but it's 5:30 in the morning and i feel lonely
and desperate. i feel like i have to solve every one of my life
problems tonight - and the sun is already up. fackles. i've
been thinking about you and i gotta say - you really are a
mystery to me - like how do you not get overwhelmed and
confused. you seem to thrive with all the constant change -
how do you do it?
all this to say: i miss you tons and pine daily for the life we
used to have. the one in which you make me laugh.

sigh.

you giant weirdo - are you googling cat stevens again?
i am alone in london now + they lost my luggage - i have
been traveling and waiting in airports for like 15 hours.
ugh. finally at london destination - chugging pimms alone in
the attic. - gawd i wish you were here.
p.s. if i have a wedding will you be my best lady ? maid of
honour sounds offensive.
i promise no creepy dresses or naked man parties or
anything.
all i want is you to know you are my favourite one in the
world. my very favourite person ever. ok ?
love you from across the ocean
exhausted.
hugs .

ohhhhhhhh - you are so sweeeeeet! of course i would be
most honoured to be your best woman (we all know that i
ain't no lady) but i will definitely be delivering a
speech. can't stop me. and what do you mean "if"?

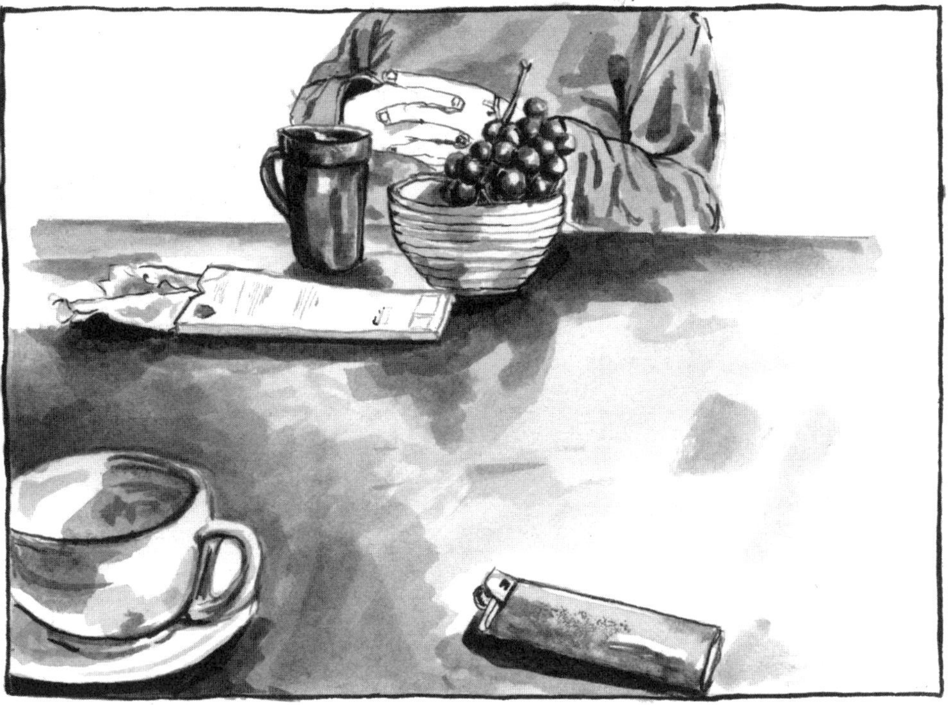

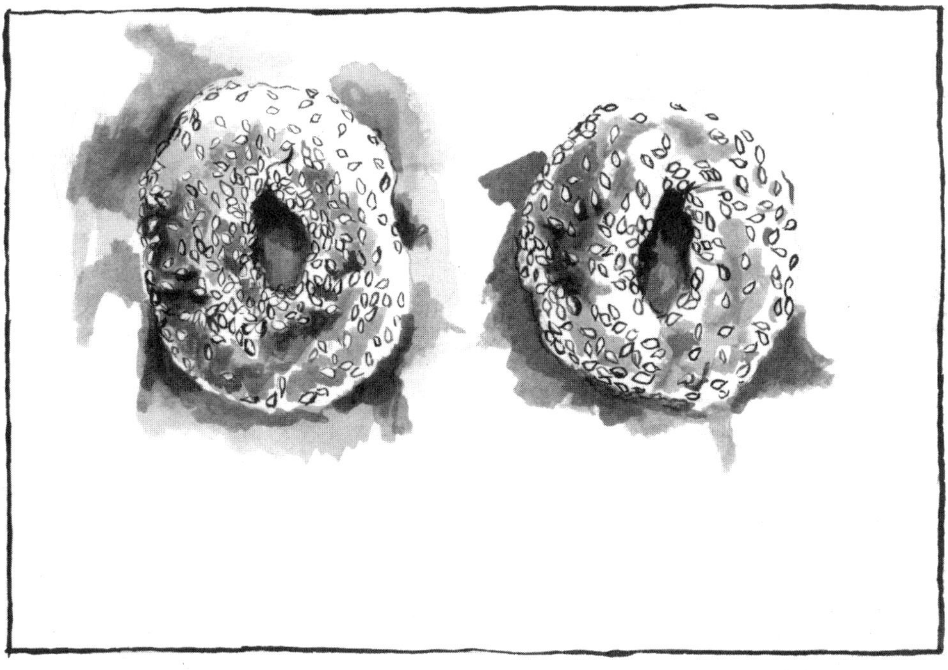

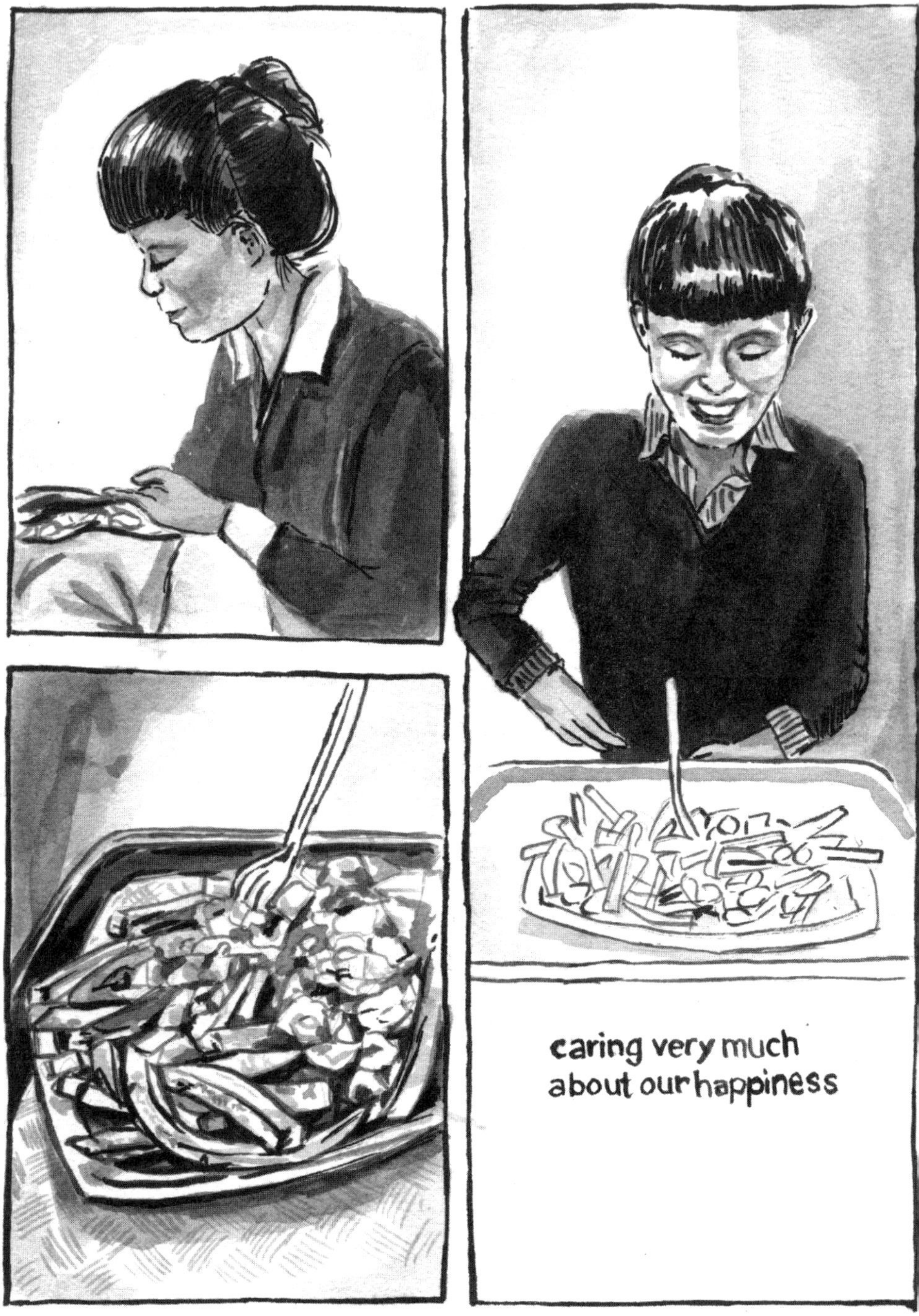
caring very much
about our happiness

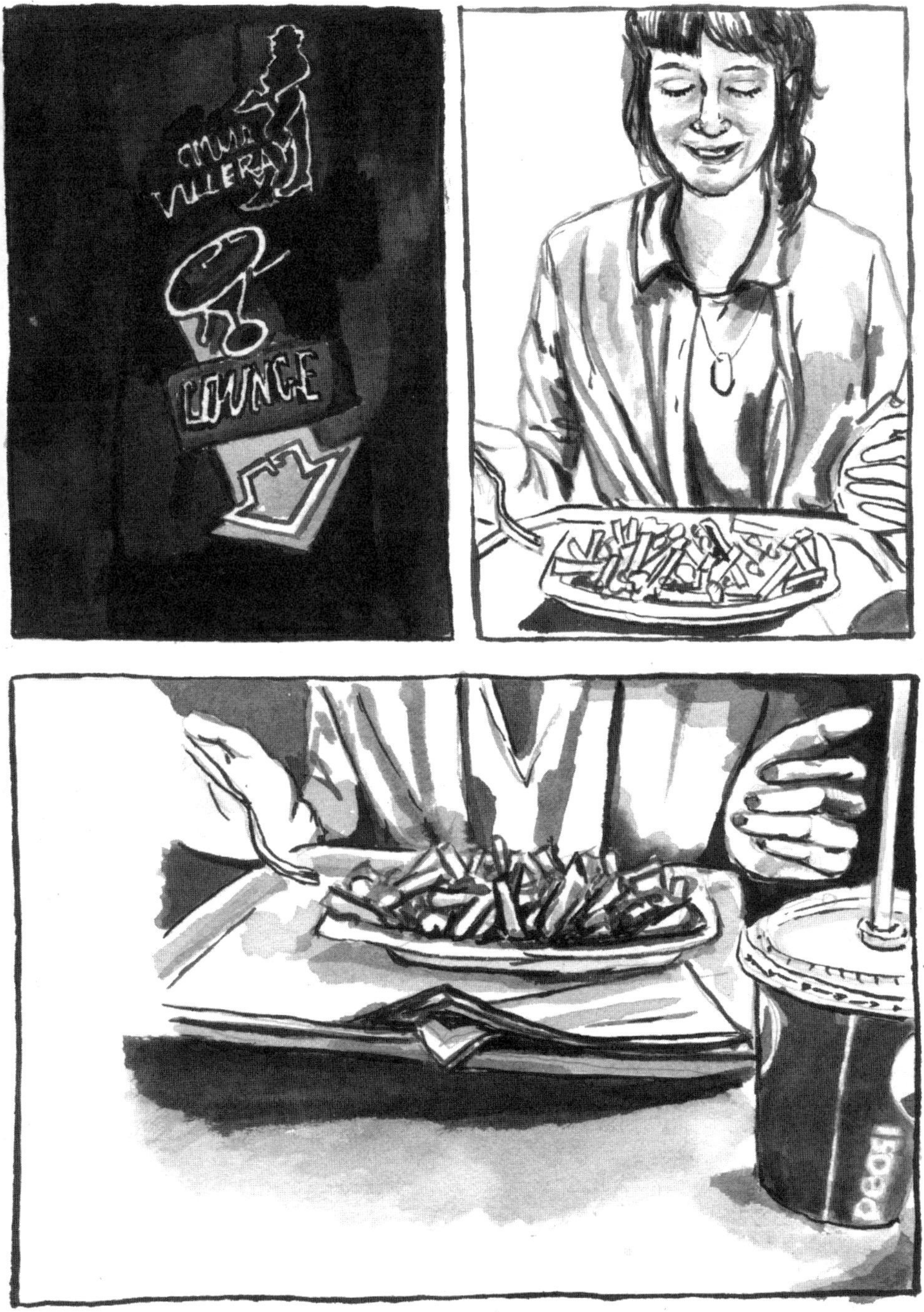
VILLERAY
LOUNGE
PEPSI

✉

i talked to F____the other day and he sounds like he's having a good time in banff but not getting much work done.
also, i think C____had his second baby - and i say that based on his girlfriend's facebook picture.

✉

things are so unfunny and lonely without you here.
i am over B____ (again) , i fell back in love with A____ for 2 days. and then he wrecked it . now i am just bored, slightly annoyed and practicing being too busy and important to give a hooten-nanny about boys. ugh. the never ending.

✉

OHHH
FUUUUUUUUUUDGE.
life is awful without you.
everyone sux or else they are totally awesome and that makes me feel bad too.
ha.
so o
R____ got the job
and i had to practice being cool and happy for her. Sad another one has to move away.
anyway that is only because my life is going nowhere -barf.

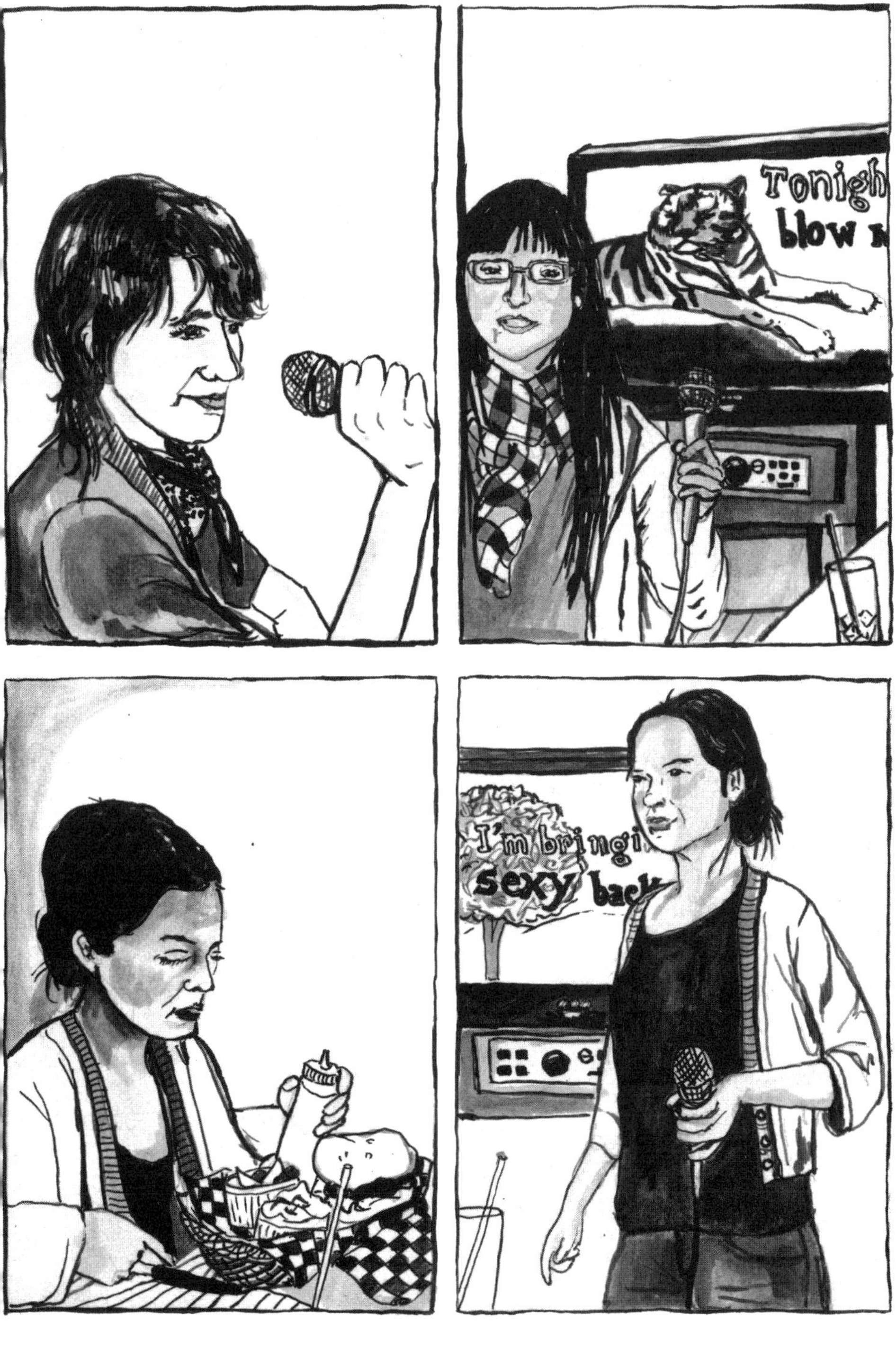
Tonigh
blow
I'm bringi
sexy bac

so...what's going on with B_____? when you say "miss
him" did you mean "mess him" - like mess him up, like
rough him up because he's such a muckefuck? i hope that's
what you meant but it was a strange typo. no really? what
is making you feel nostalgic for him? please
remember that you're basically trapped on a desert island
with 30 artists
i can't wait for this stupid cleanse to be done. i'm
basically just trying to satiate myself with various nut butters
and getting really fat doing it.

what the heck – B_____! a hug? i hope it was
clothed. ohmygod this must be so strange and emotional
for you. how are you dealing with it? how did this come
out? i'm surprised that he would make himself so
vulnerable by telling you that. wow. crazy. i would hate to
be C_____ right now. i need more details.
i guess A_____'s opening was tonight? i missed it. at
home. with my weird condition.

hey dude +
i love you .
D_____ is leaving tomorrow
i am in a bit of shock re my life .
what am i doing etc. etc. etc.
also went to doctor again today - and they did a
leap - which is totally freaky way to start the day.
awesome.
D_____ is currently playing scrabble on line with his ex.
and then we are going to drink wine.

this morning A_____ and i had an enormous blowout and broke up in his
SUV
he threatened to marry me as a punishment - it was so
ridiculous. we yelled at each other for 2 hours pulled over on the
street.
now he just keeps saying how i wrecked everything and how he was
"going" to marry me blah blah. it's a mess.
i learned that at best i can only go to states twice for 6 months if i am
lucky. now i am freaking out and have to start re-applying for teaching
jobs all over again.
how do you feel about waterloo? they are hiring. wanna live in
waterloo? with me?
geezus.
Quelle désastre.

happy to have a month in sackville to figure out what to do with my future + i am babysitting a very old dog, 2 cats and 4 hens and a rooster. The poultry kinda freak me out .

my mom is coming over tonight to hang out - which is really exciting, i miss stability so much that suddenly just the idea of having a mom seems like the most certain and amazingly nice thing. whew.

how are things shaping up for that hippie art residency ? i feel like you will go there . you will be loved and cherished and then will end up running the whole place, i picture you spinning vases bare foot eating quinoa with a baby strapped on your back in a leather satchel. is that your plan? it's ok with me. i would really like to see you have dreadlocks finally.

p.s. just to be super clear - just because A___ and i got engaged does not mean we are having babies definitely no babies. We want to have studios and Europe. we decided to leave it an open discussion and reassess in four years.

also any ideas how to go about having a wedding? Are we catholic?, i'm such a fraud.

i don't even know what city? summer ?

N.B.? MTL? Surely we will have problems with the border, we have about $100 to spend on it . i can't make sense of anything without you. you and kuchen. please get here . . .

sorry this is so long, its quiet out here.

i been alone soo o o o long.

my biggest love to you,

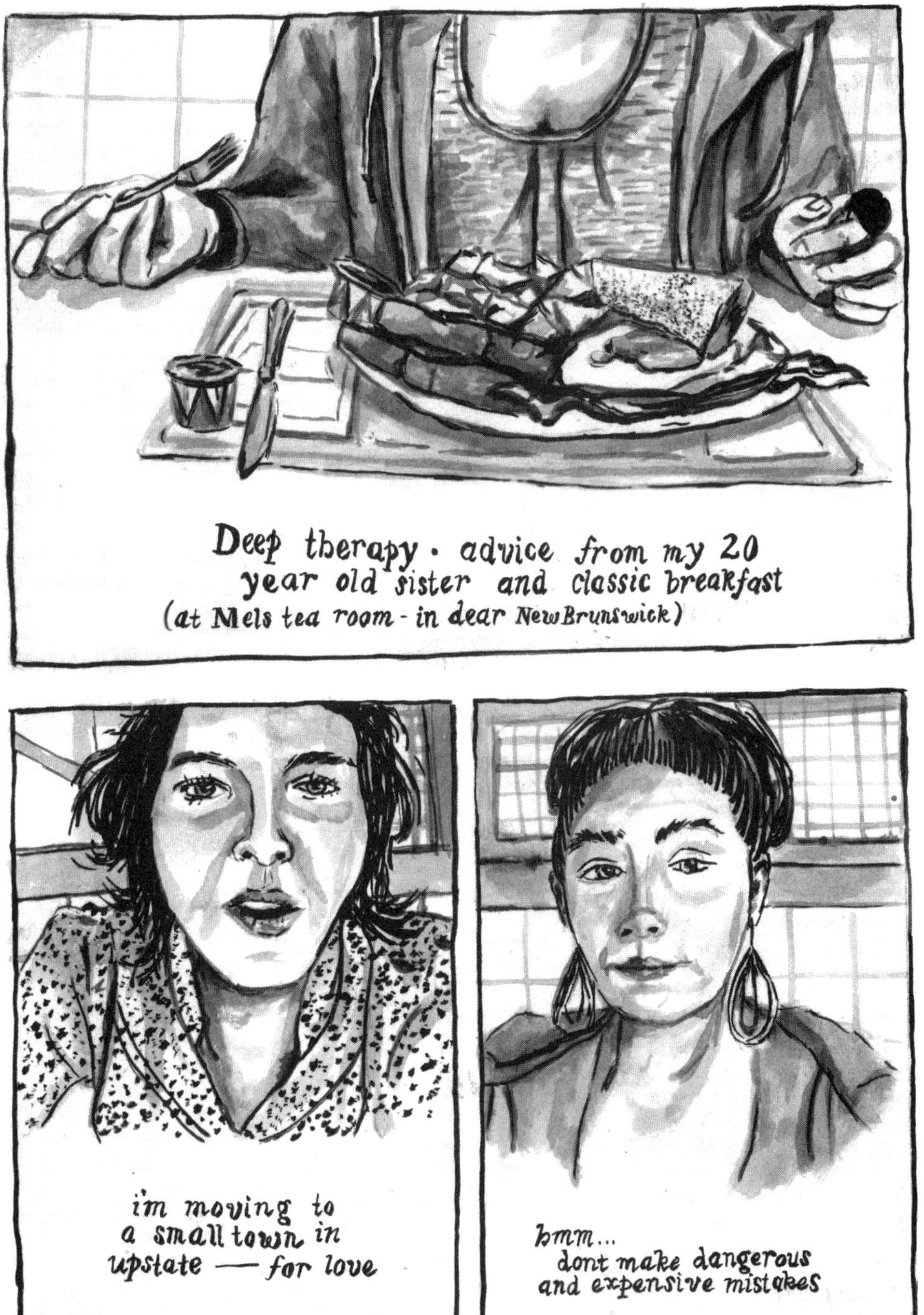
Deep therapy • advice from my 20 year old sister and classic breakfast
(at Mels tea room - in dear NewBrunswick)
i'm moving to a smalltown in upstate — for love
hmm...
dont make dangerous and expensive mistakes

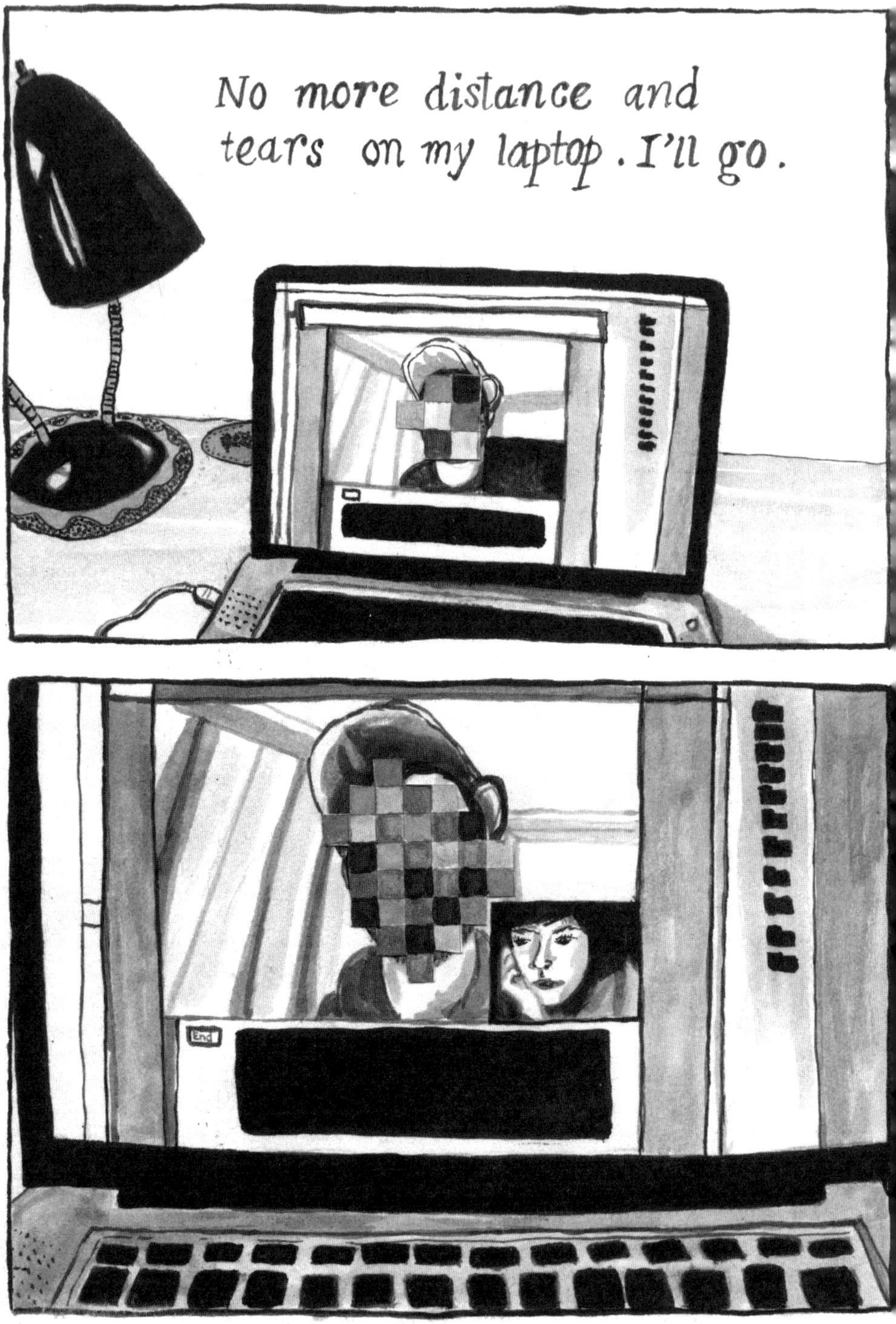
No more distance and tears on my laptop. I'll go.
End

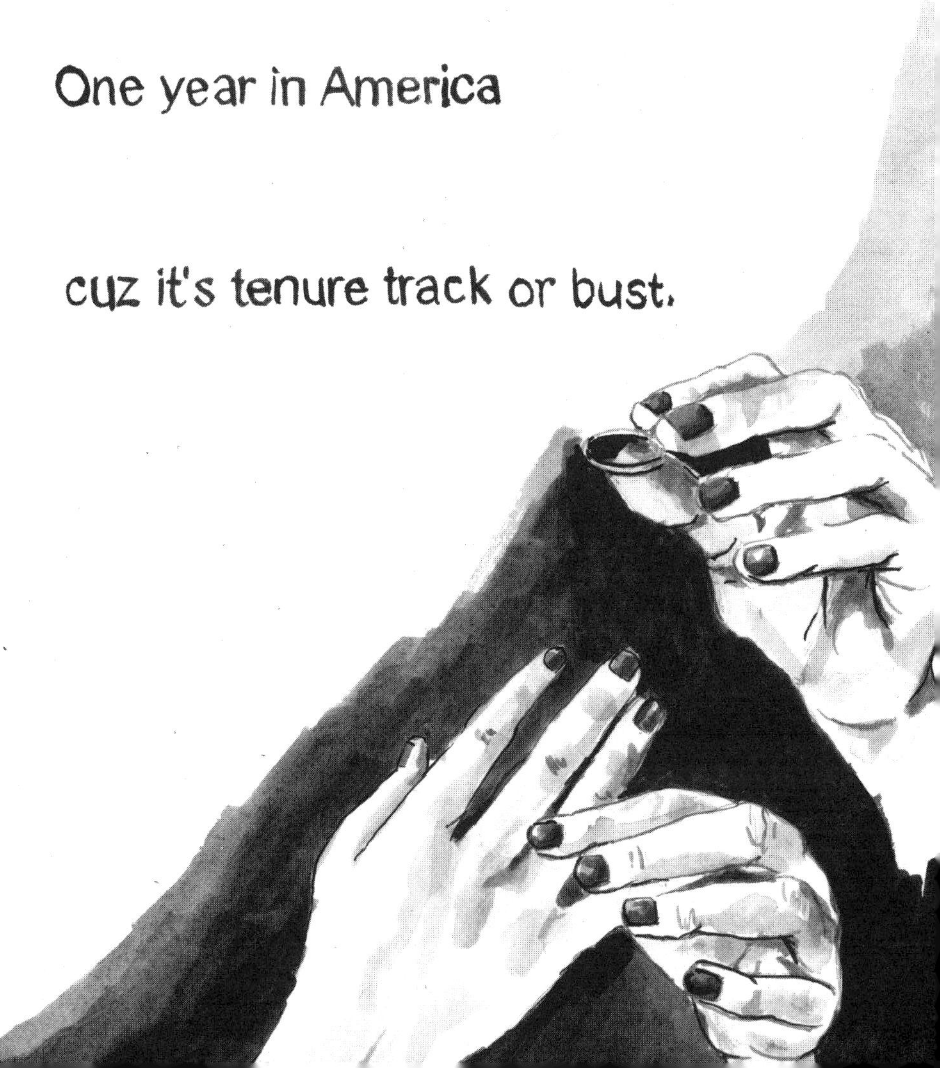
One year in America
cuz it's tenure track or bust.

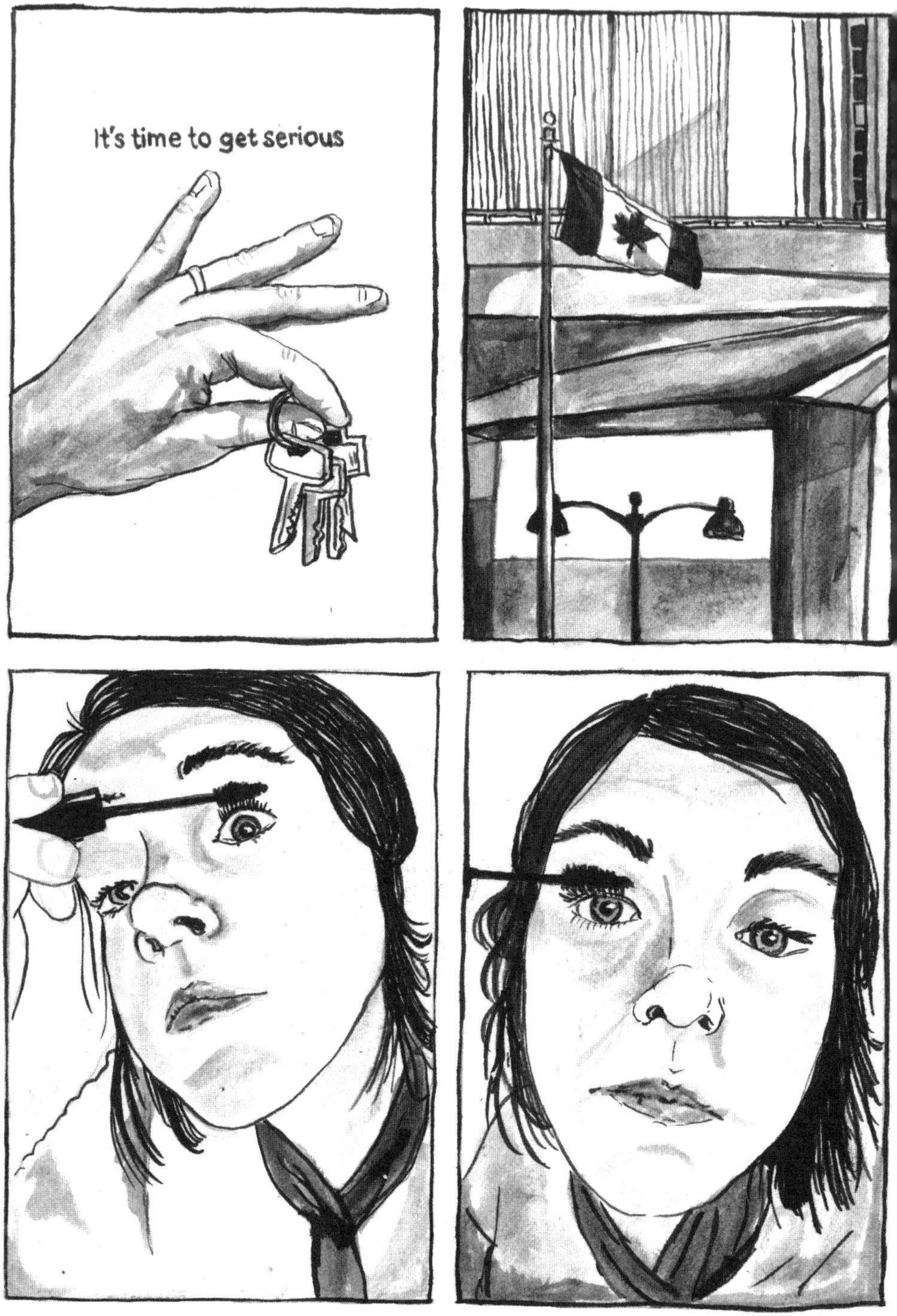
It's time to get serious

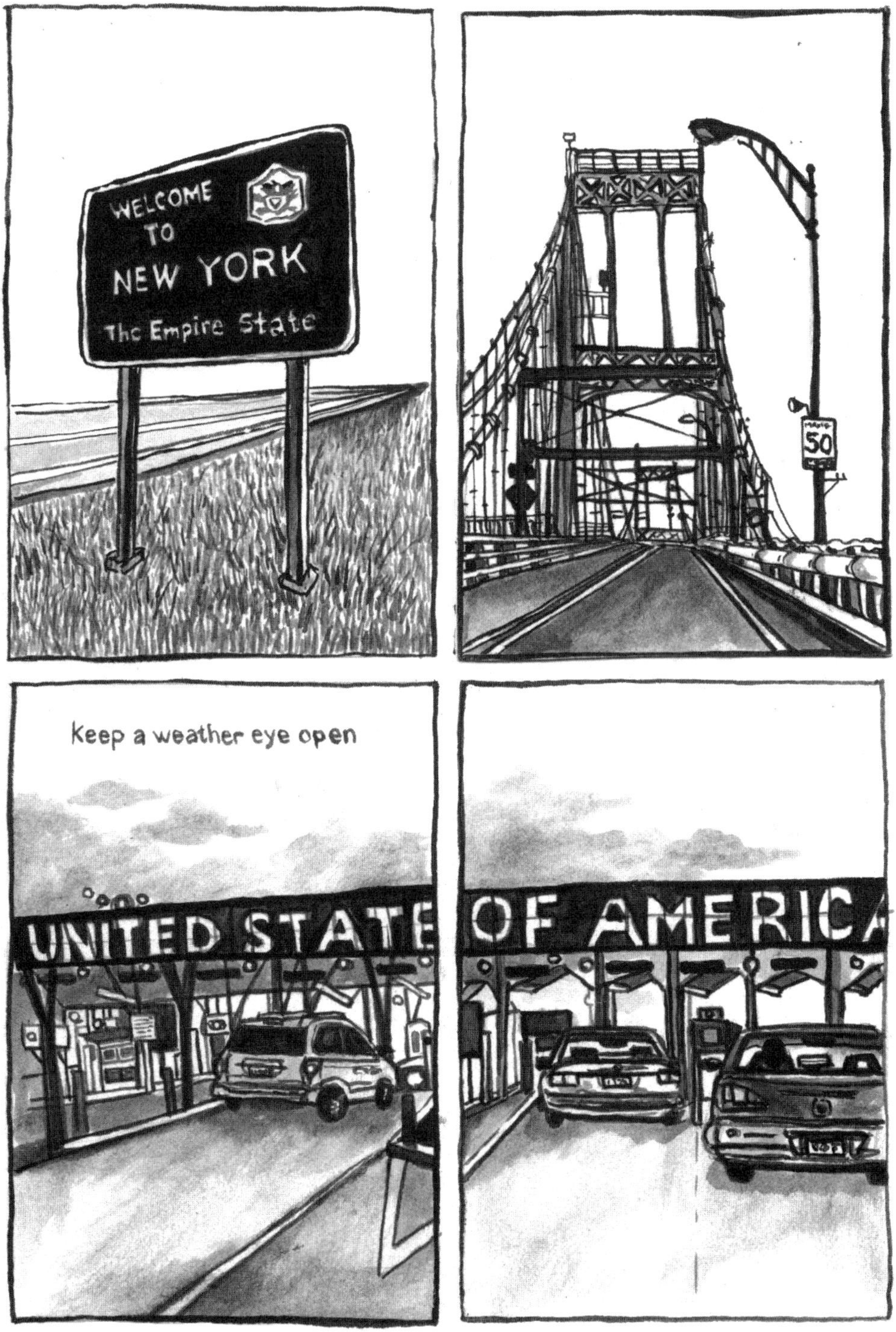
WELCOME
TO
NEW YORK
The Empire State
50
Keep a weather eye open
UNITED STATE
OF AMERICA

▼

oh.........what the hell am i gonna do here without you? i
can't believe you secret cried on the plane. that's so
sad. your desk looks really lonely and D____ misses you -
he is boiling his broccoli in the kitchen right now.

▼

i can't believe you skype slept with E____- that is so
sweet. and also heartbreaking. and HE said he didn't want
a long-distance relationship.
how's the london limbo? I have so much to tell you, i'm just
going to dive right in:

1. I got BUSTED by the metro cops today and it was
horrible. it wouldn't have been so bad if i didn't try to run
from them
:)
:)
:)
ah well, vhatever, so i'm 40 bucks poorer and really
embarrassed.

▼

You have been super solidly in love for so long- i am
officially used to thinking of him as your red
boyfriend. A___and I found an apartment - we move in
August - unless i get a magic job in Canada and then who
knows... we are making manicotti for dinner i am gonna
have a period - i feel crazy and fat and sad but hyper. ...
you know ?
The kids at Cornell finish school this week so the frat
houses are partying like crazy we can hear them all over
town from the hills. Party tents - police sirens
drunk girls and american money falling from the sky.
this place is crazy.

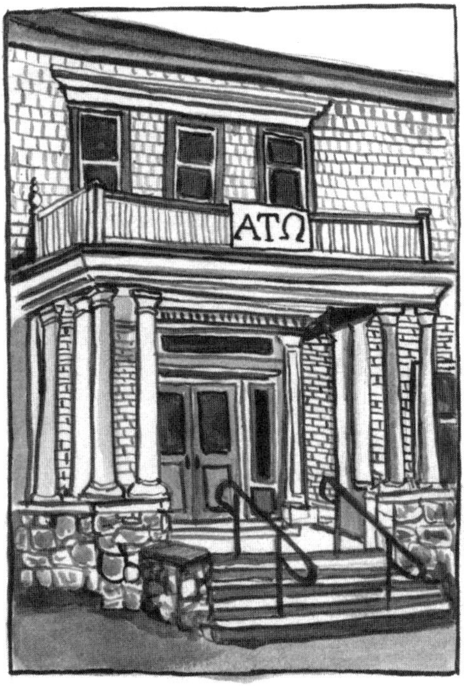
ΑΤΩ

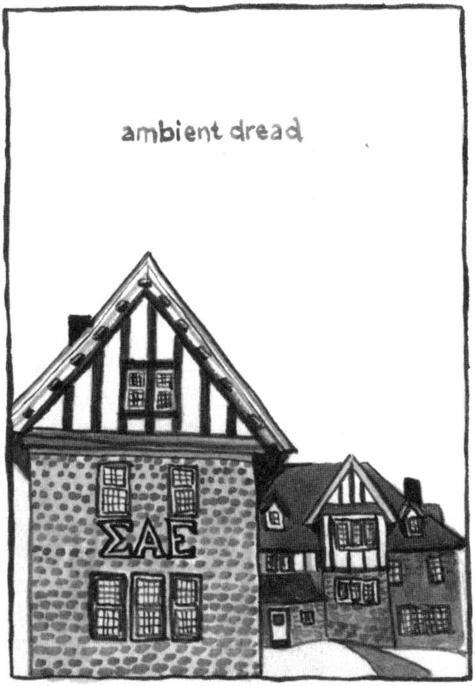
ambient dread
ΣΑΕ

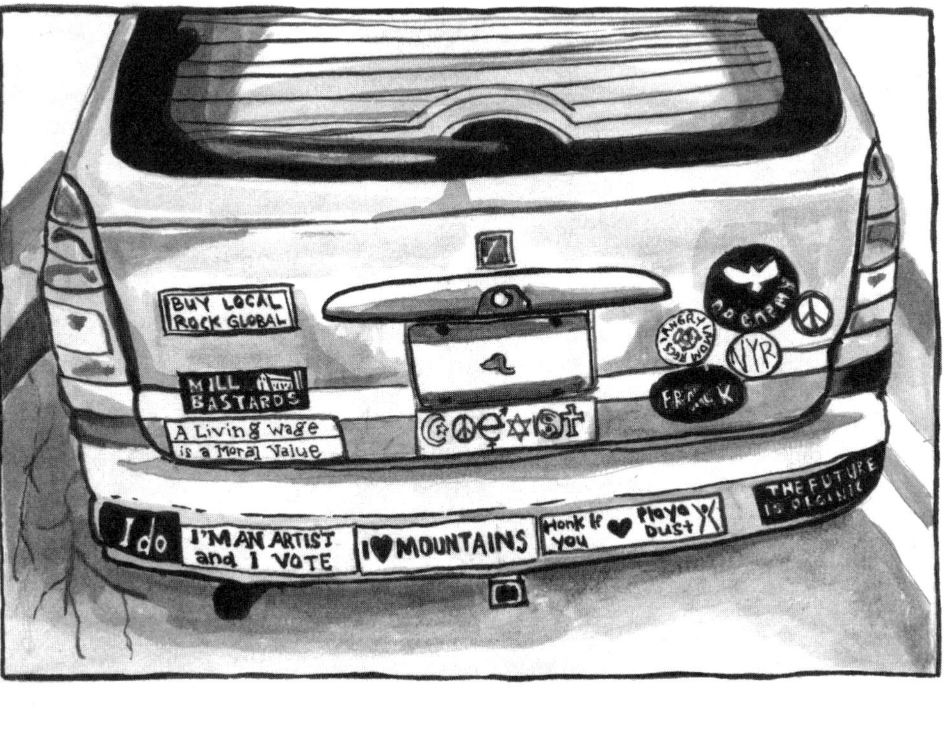
BUY LOCAL ROCK GLOBAL
MILL BASTARDS
A Living wage is a Moral Value
NYR
I do
I'M AN ARTIST and I VOTE
I ♥ MOUNTAINS
Honk if you ♥ Playa Dust
THE FUTURE IS ORGANIC

▼

fact: cyber sex can be good – B____ and i proved that.
ugh . your right i am not in love with B_____ .
i am in love with this residency- it makes me so sad that it will ever end
- i can't even think about it.
i feel terrible about sending B_____ that e-mail – I worry that there.
will be repercussions . i actually got so wasted and like in a bad
movie i woke up hungover this morning and lived for about 10
minutes before remembering what i did last night and basically
stopped dead and swore out loud and felt the shame all day. .

▼

i tried to suggest to A_____ about going to berlin - berlin would
mean leaving A_____ probably. can you come here to help this
decision with me? i need you for the laughing and i think you are
probably working too hard. where did your tonsillitis go are you okay
? i can't see the future any more
lastly - i am staying an extra week at the residency because my book
is taking longer than expected .. i love it here and i am dreading
_____ with all my heart.

▼

there is so much i want to talk to you about - like MONTREAL ? are
you sure ? you really want to live there for good?
why not berlin ?
i need to talk to you before i get married .. if i get married. it must be
sad packing all your things again.

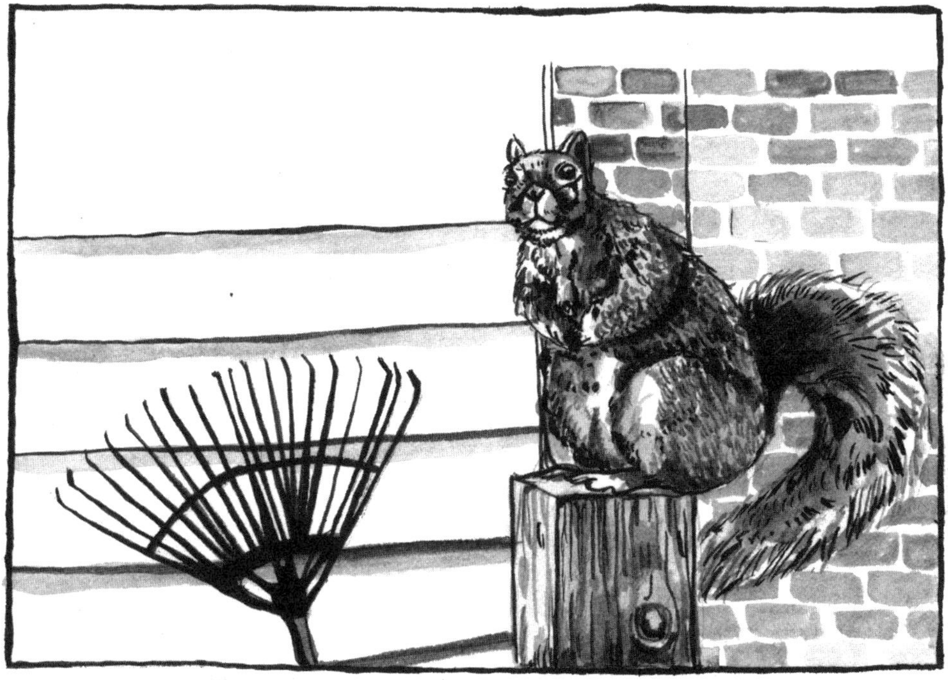

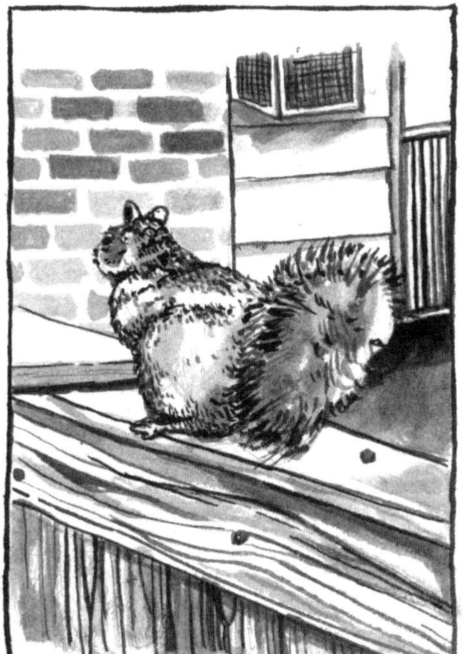

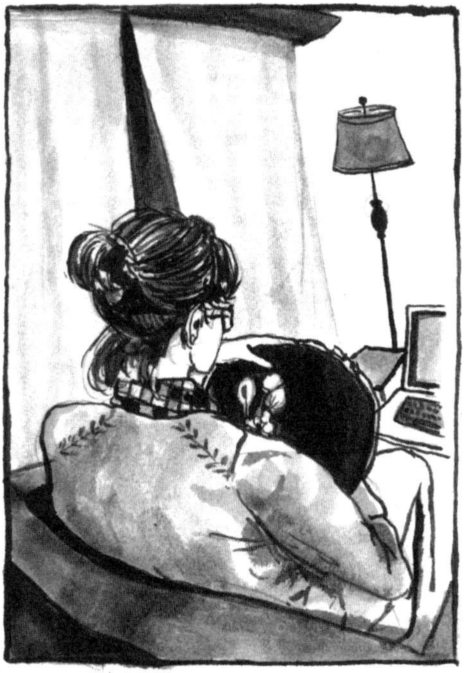

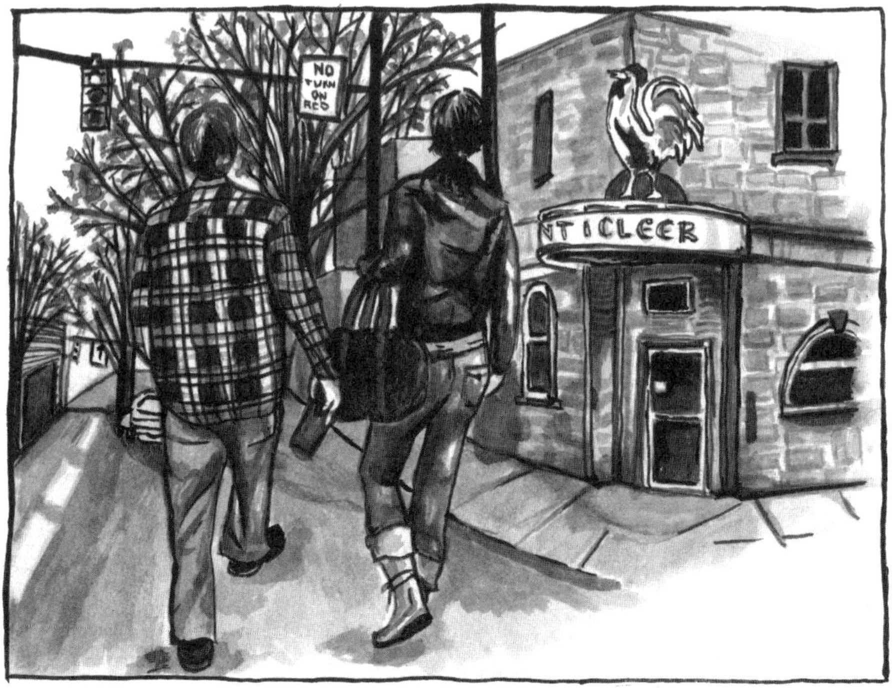
NO TURN ON RED
NTICLEER

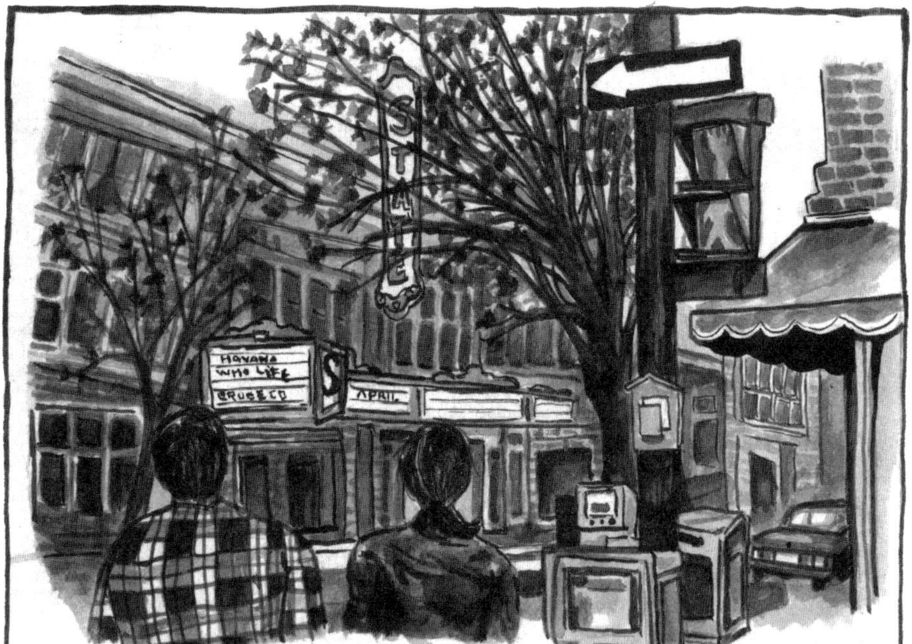
HAVANA
APRIL

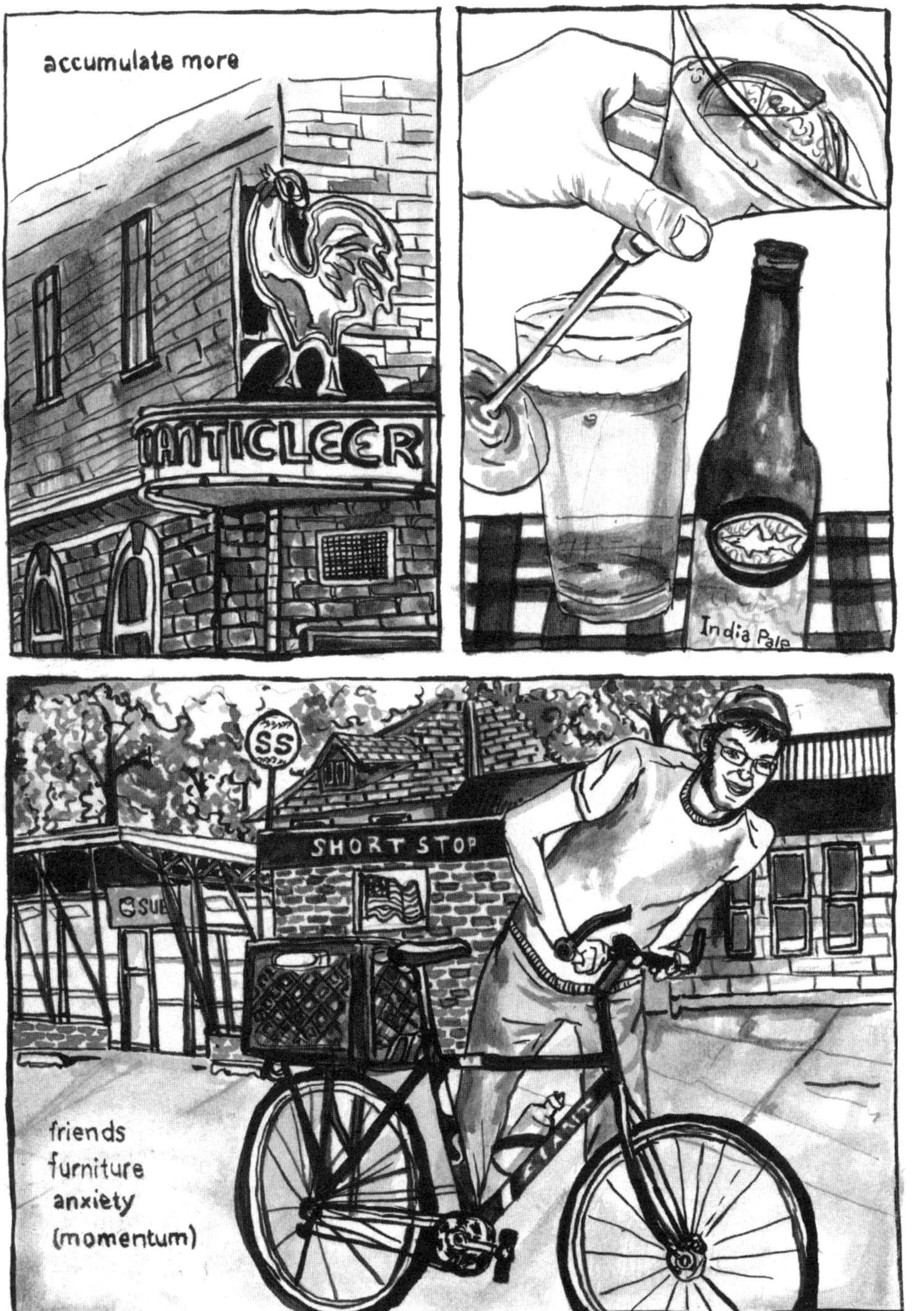
accumulate more
ANTICLEER
India Pale
SS
SHORT STOP
friends
furniture
anxiety
(momentum)

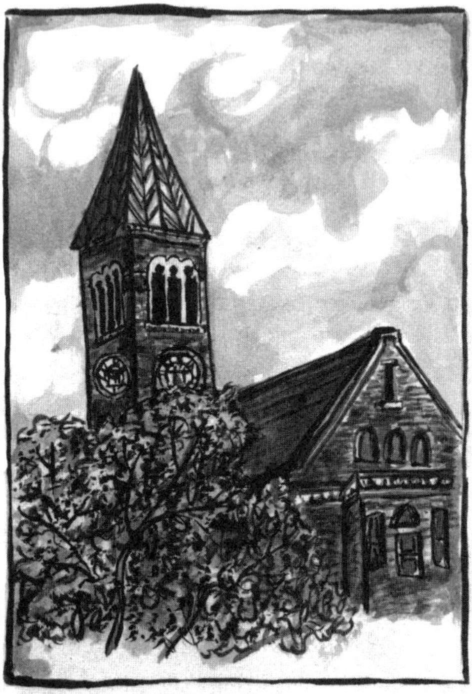

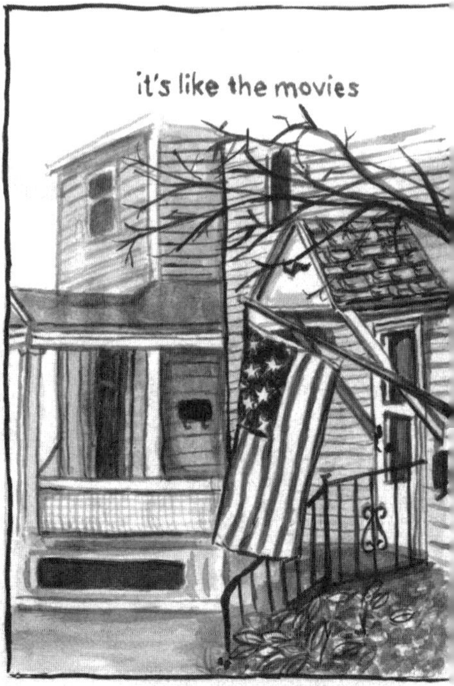
it's like the movies

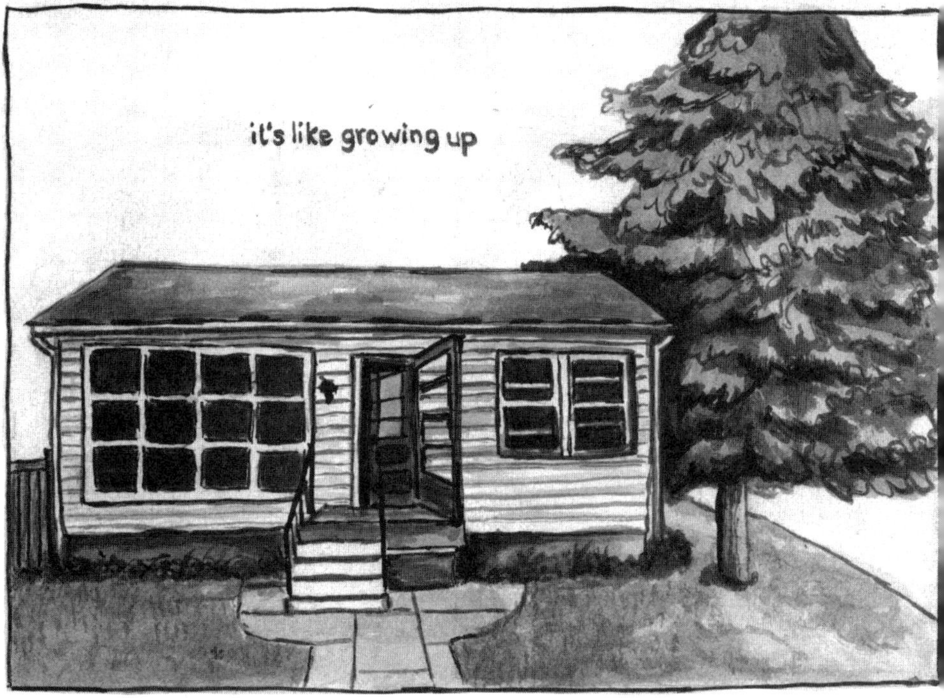
it's like growing up

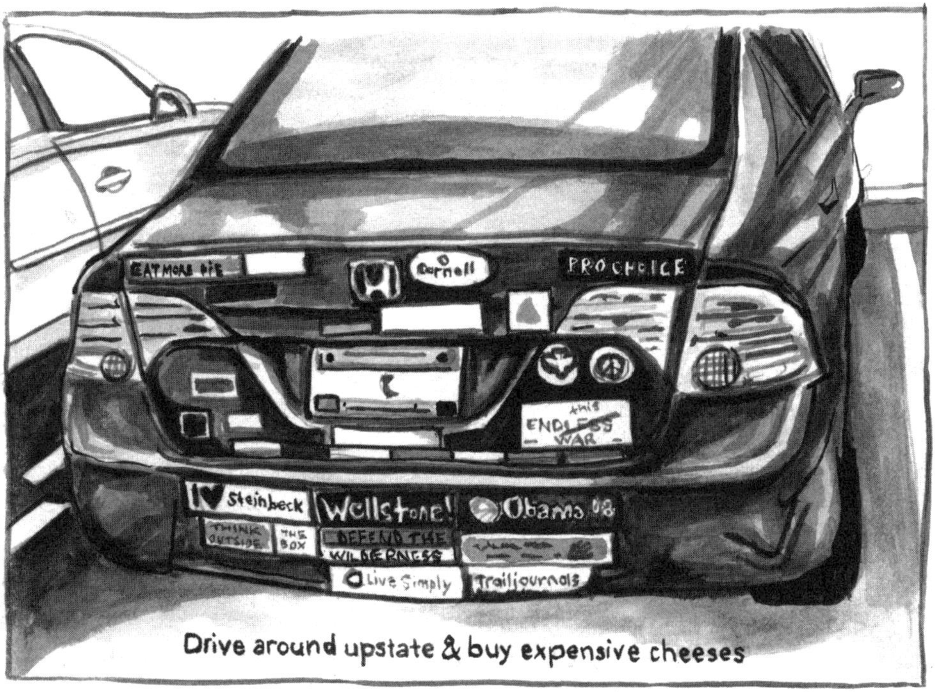
EAT MORE PIE
Cornell
PRO CHOICE
this ENDLESS WAR
I ♥ Steinbeck
Wellstone!
Obama 08
THINK OUTSIDE THE BOX
DEFEND THE WILDERNESS
Live Simply
Trailjournals
Drive around upstate & buy expensive cheeses

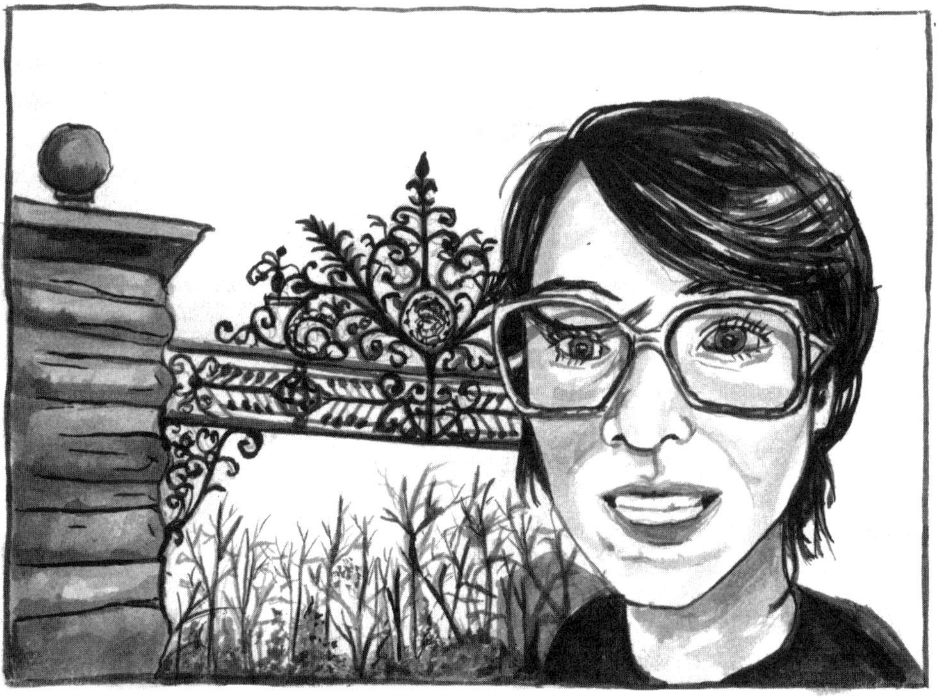

married people breakfast

a complete story has a

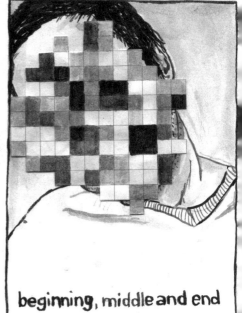

beginning, middle and end

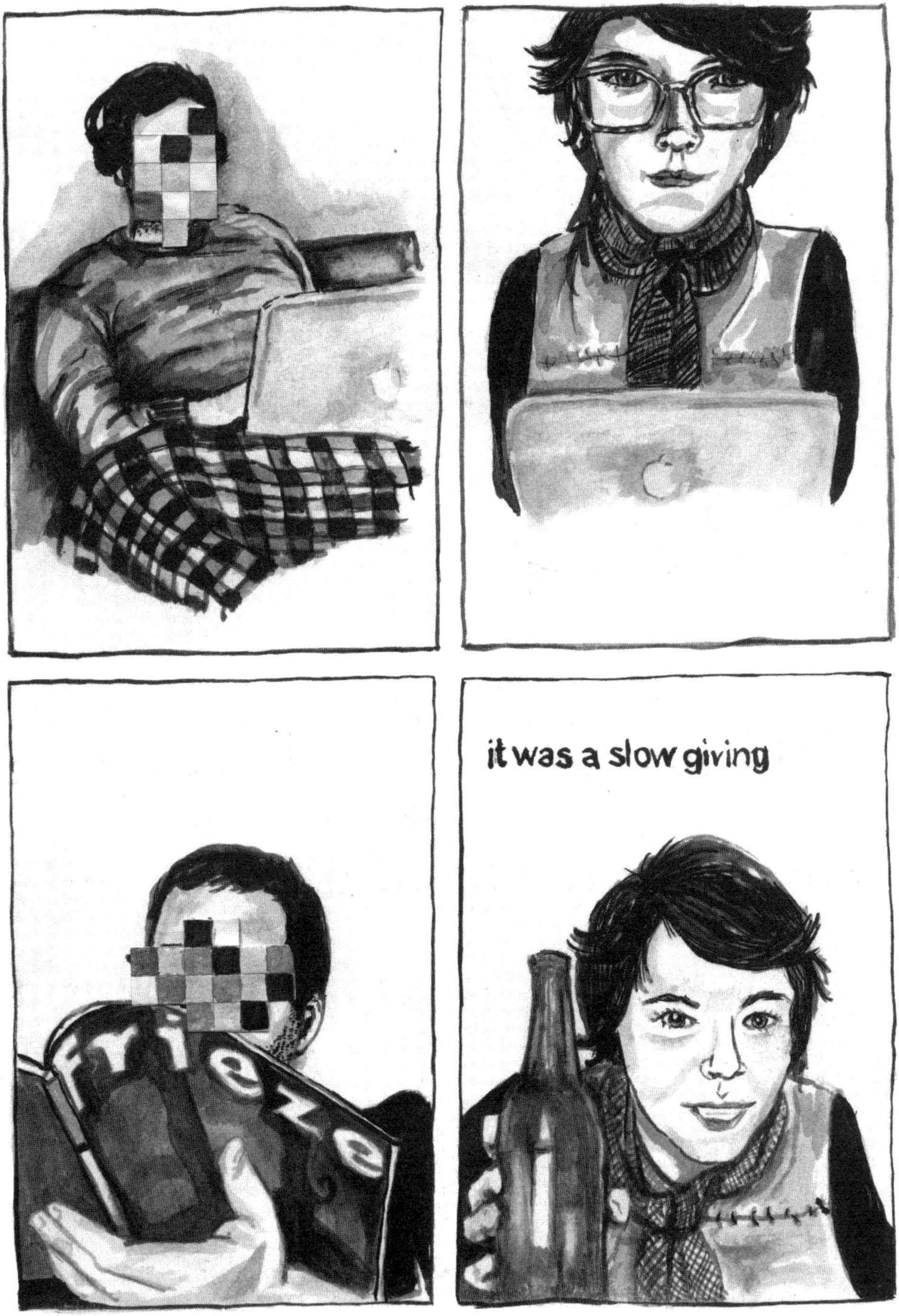
frieze
it was a slow giving

so my shining new computer arrived by a french fed-ex man in a blizzard and that was great - and then i had to contact my web server to give them the new coordinates etc. and then i erased my whole website by accident . cool huh ?

so now at least i have something to keep me busy - plus i have an ongoing battle with Koodo that has now gone to the better business bureau and that is also really fun times. ugh. but i just ate about 4 litres of cheesy pasta - so i am feeling pretty good except i have another ovarian cyst - totally amazing - so when i have a full stomach it kills.

totally uninspired to make any art but i picked up a sweet copy of the history of the group of seven. yup seriously from the Art gallery of Ontario when i went a few weeks ago. so i plan to curl up around my cyst and read tonight in my 480 square foot home. you should come visit me - if you aren't working - come here and let's make a collaboration art work thingy, please. OH AND YOUR EGGS. yes this is important. on a scale of 1-10 how serious are you about having a baby ?

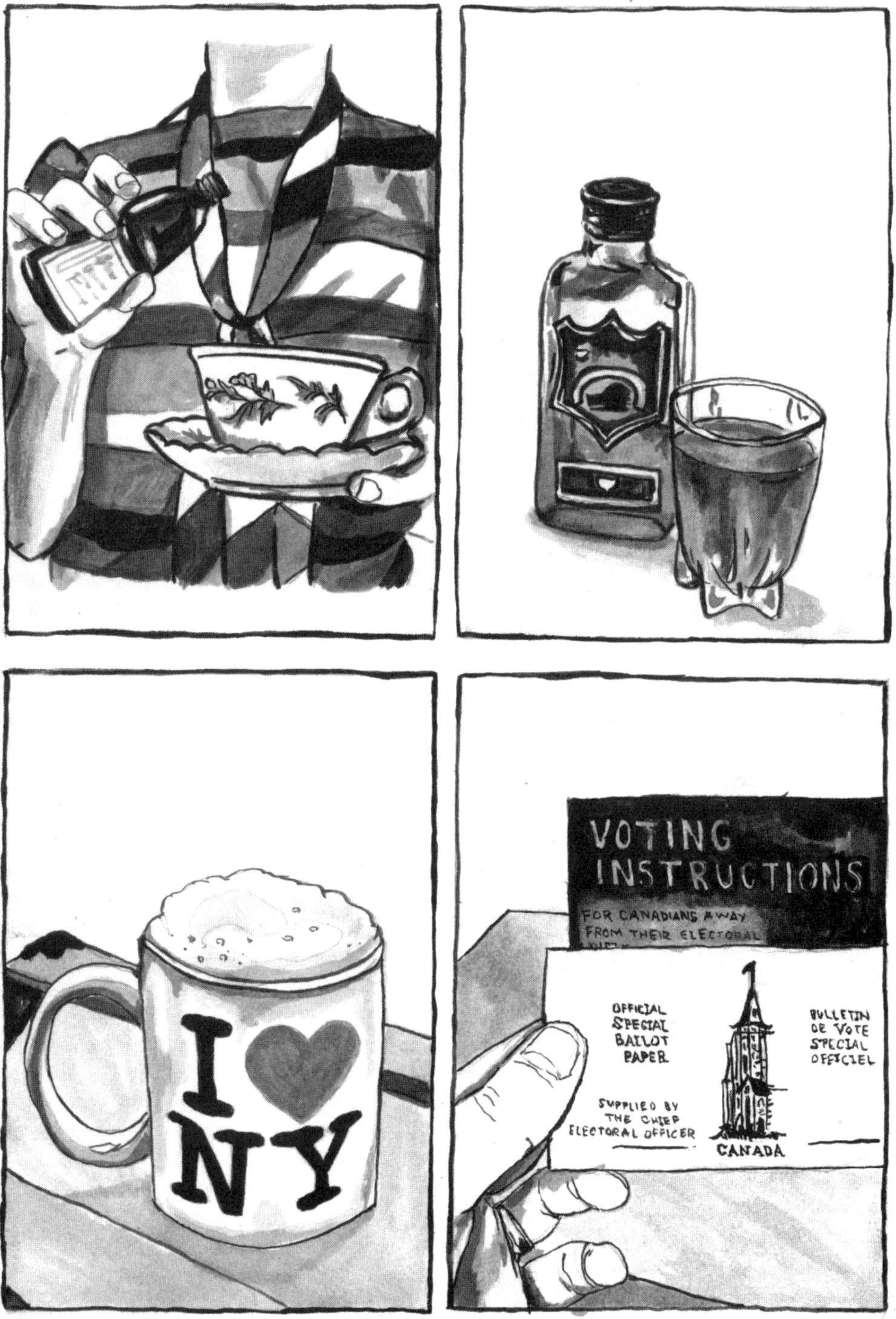
I ♥ NY
VOTING INSTRUCTIONS
FOR CANADIANS AWAY FROM THEIR ELECTORAL
OFFICIAL SPECIAL BALLOT PAPER
BULLETIN DE VOTE SPECIAL OFFICIEL
SUPPLIED BY THE CHIEF ELECTORAL OFFICER
CANADA

oh you +
how are YOU ?
i think about you everyday , and if i do not write it is because my life is
shamefully boring +
being in america makes me worry about being lower middle class and
aging. just like that- i became way more politically engaged, started
caring ALOT about the long gun registry and fears of canada being
taken over in the dark of night. i stream cbc all day long, pretending i
am actually still in mtl, flying into rages about Harper's new eye
glasses and his terrible french accent. today cbc said that women in
montreal have more sex than women in toronto or vancouver. i made
pesto yesterday. today i saw a picture of A_____'s grandpa on the
refrigerator and had a devastating urge to have a baby - like right now
. i think i am going crazy - never leave me alone again. i have been
incredibly depressed for the last month- since leaving montreal. i am
doing okay- at least now i want to stop being depressed - instead of
just wanting to die. that is good. i actually enjoyed coffee today.. i feel
like the residency will change all this.
Ok gotta go the hippies are building something out front, it involves
styrofoam. oh dear.
XO

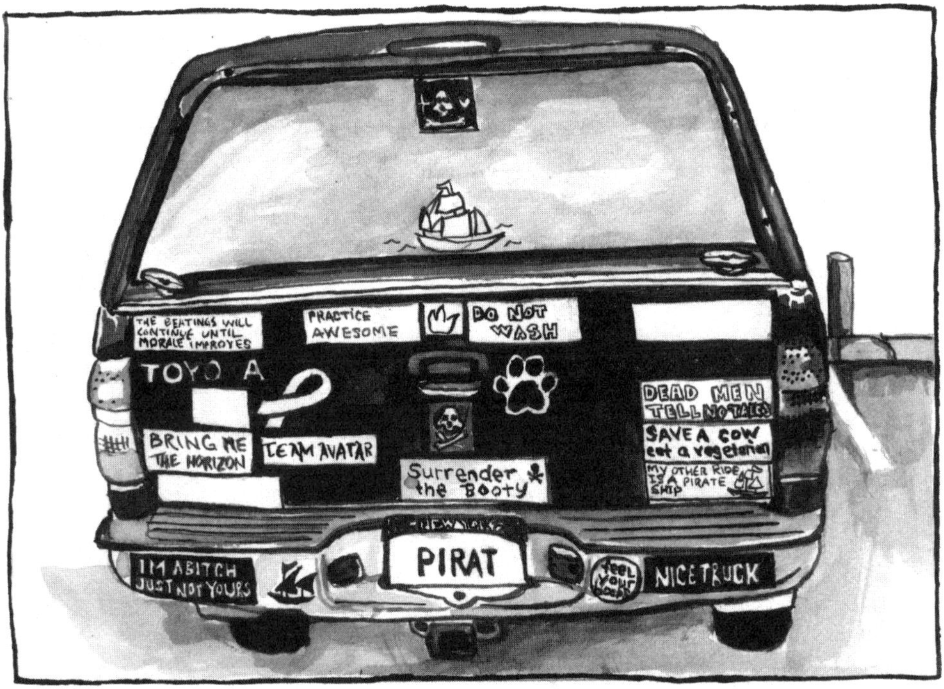
THE BEATINGS WILL CONTINUE UNTIL MORALE IMPROVES
PRACTICE AWESOME
DO NOT WASH
TOYO A
DEAD MEN TELL NO TALES
BRING ME THE HORIZON
TEAM AVATAR
SAVE A COW eat a vegetarian
MY OTHER RIDE IS A PIRATE SHIP
Surrender the Booty
NEW YORK
PIRAT
IM A BITCH JUST NOT YOURS
feel your beat
NICETRUCK

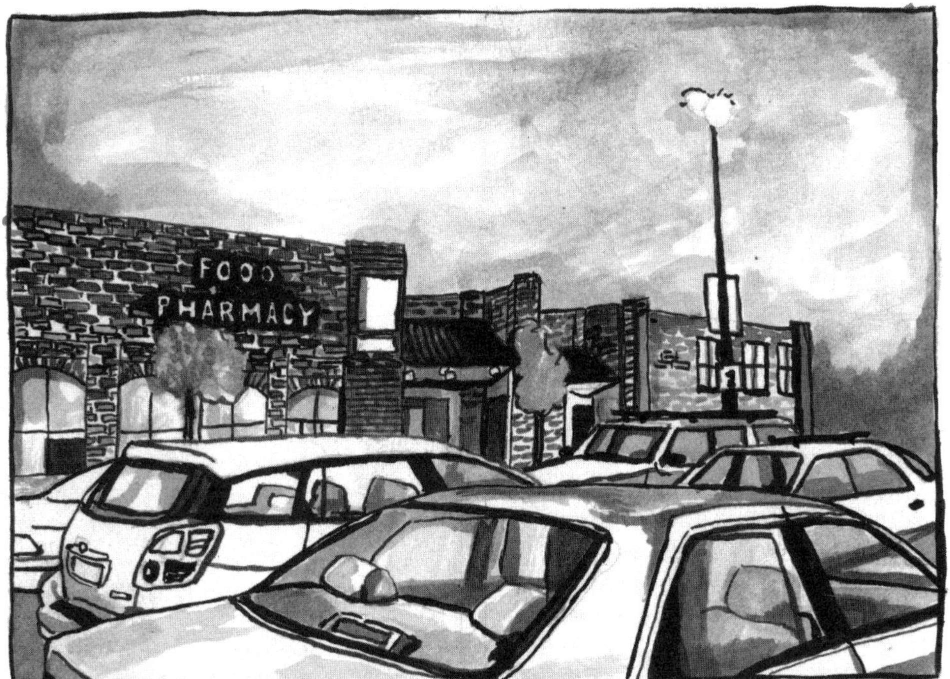
FOOD
PHARMACY

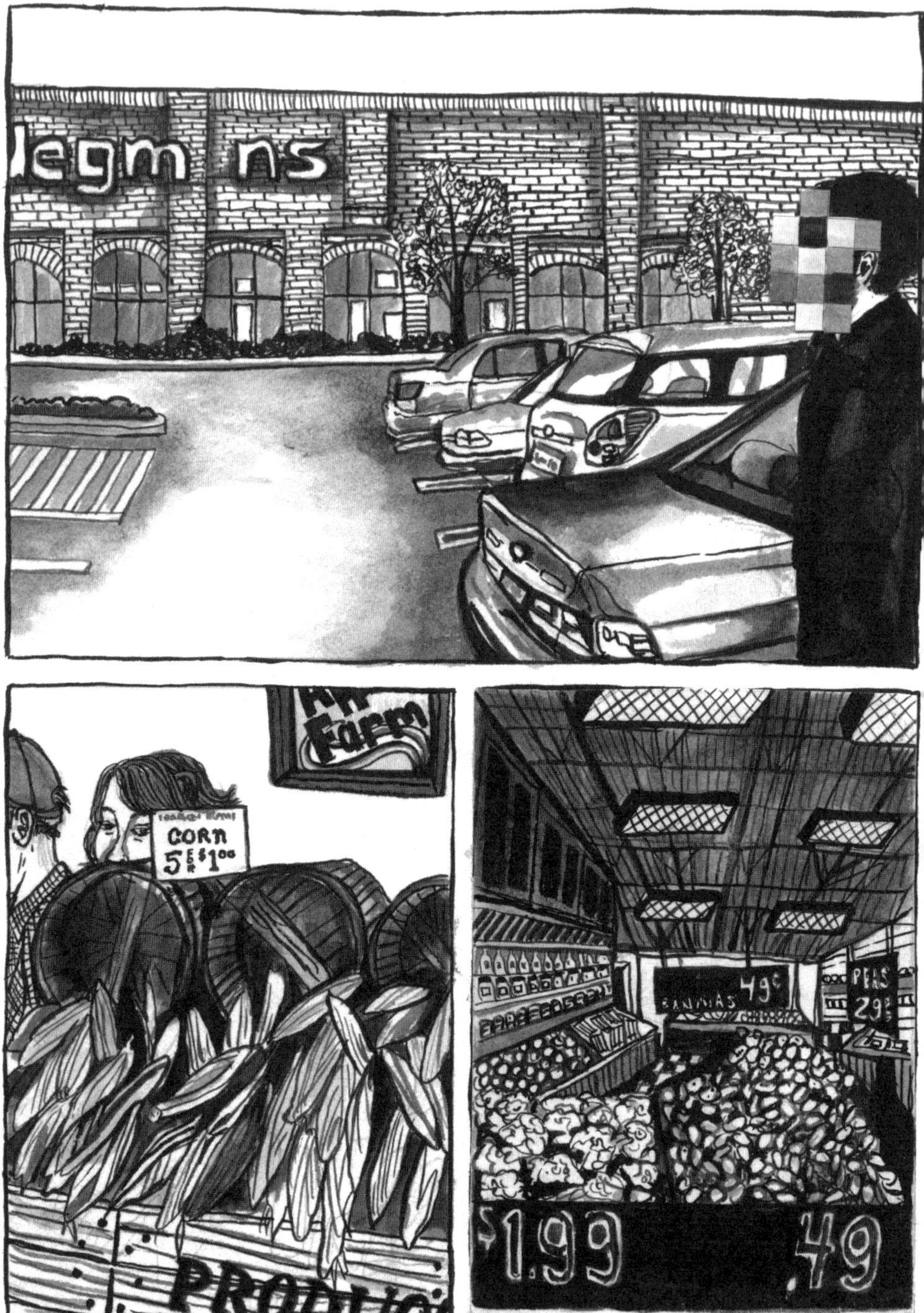
legm ns
Farm
CORN
5 FOR $1.00
PRODUC
BANANAS 49¢
PEARS 29¢
$1.99
.49

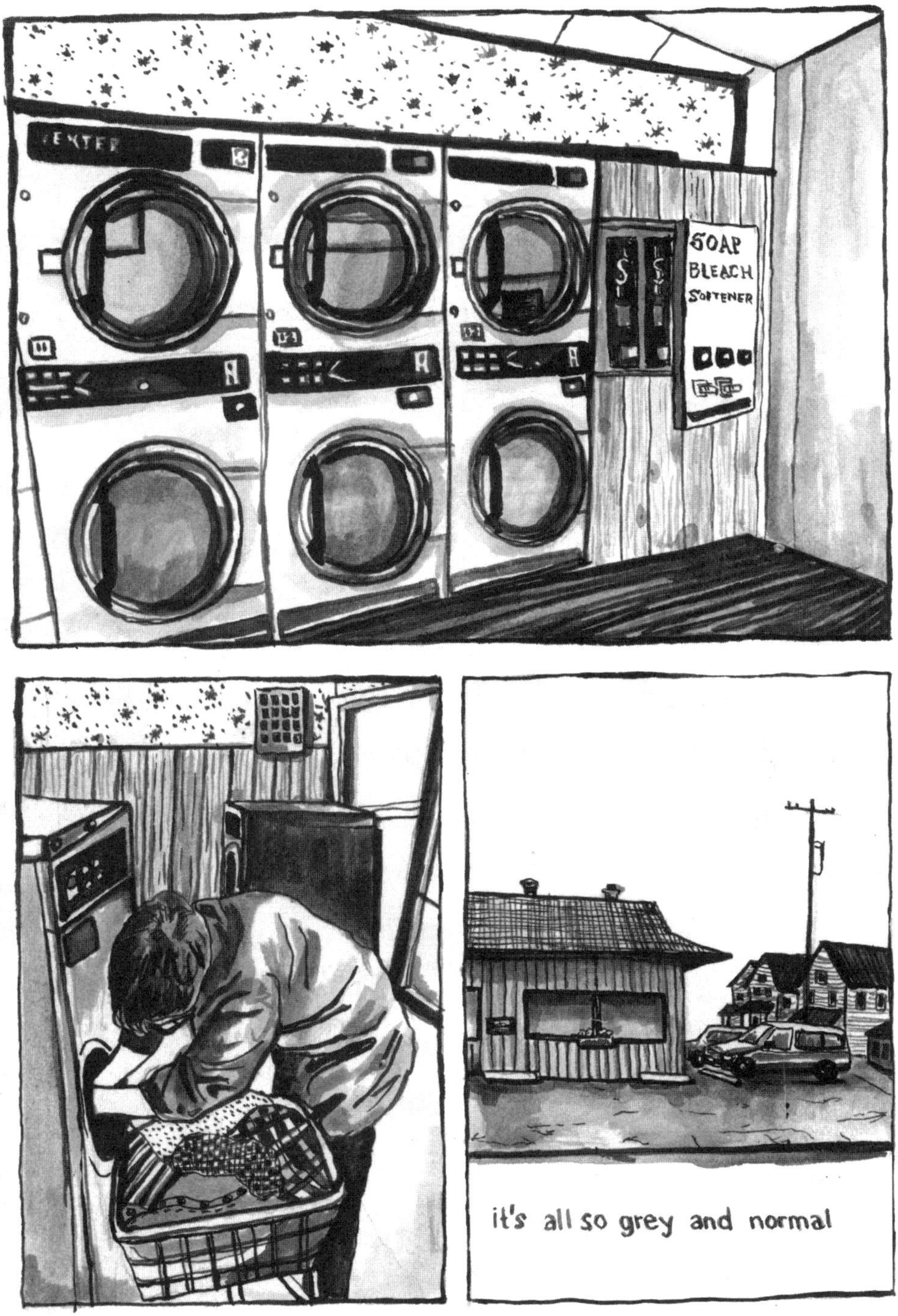
SOAP
BLEACH
SOFTENER
it's all so grey and normal

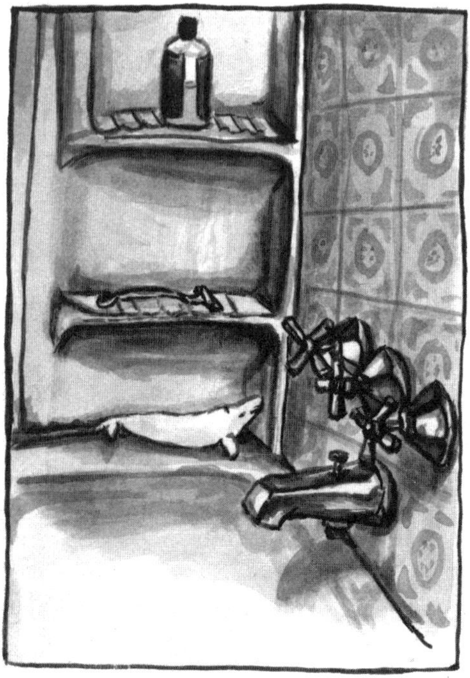

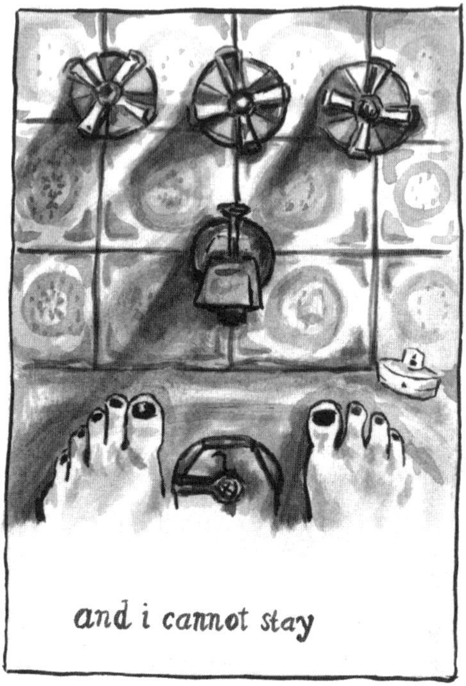
and i cannot stay

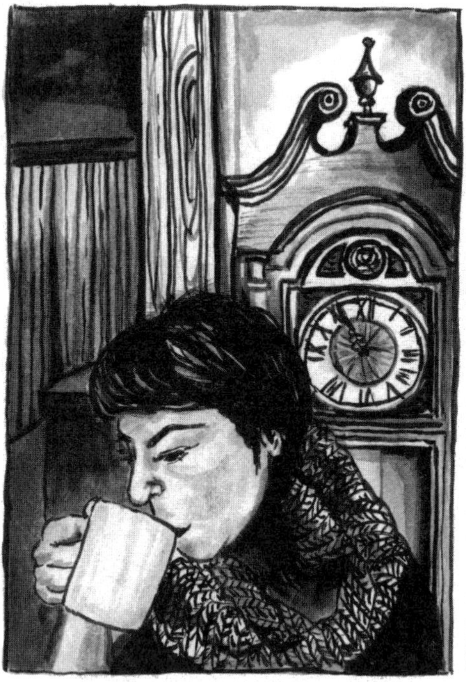

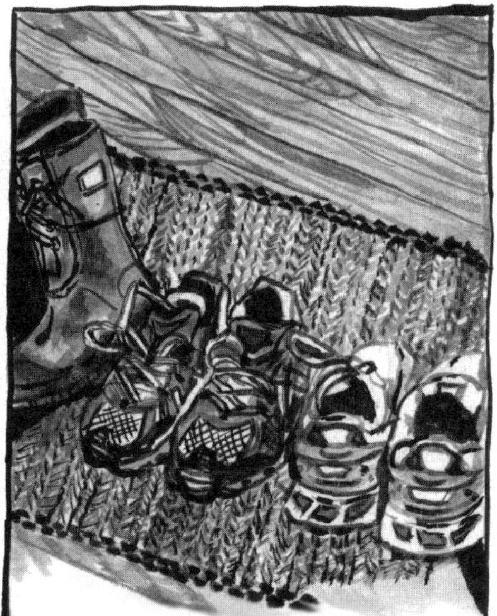
RUN back HOME

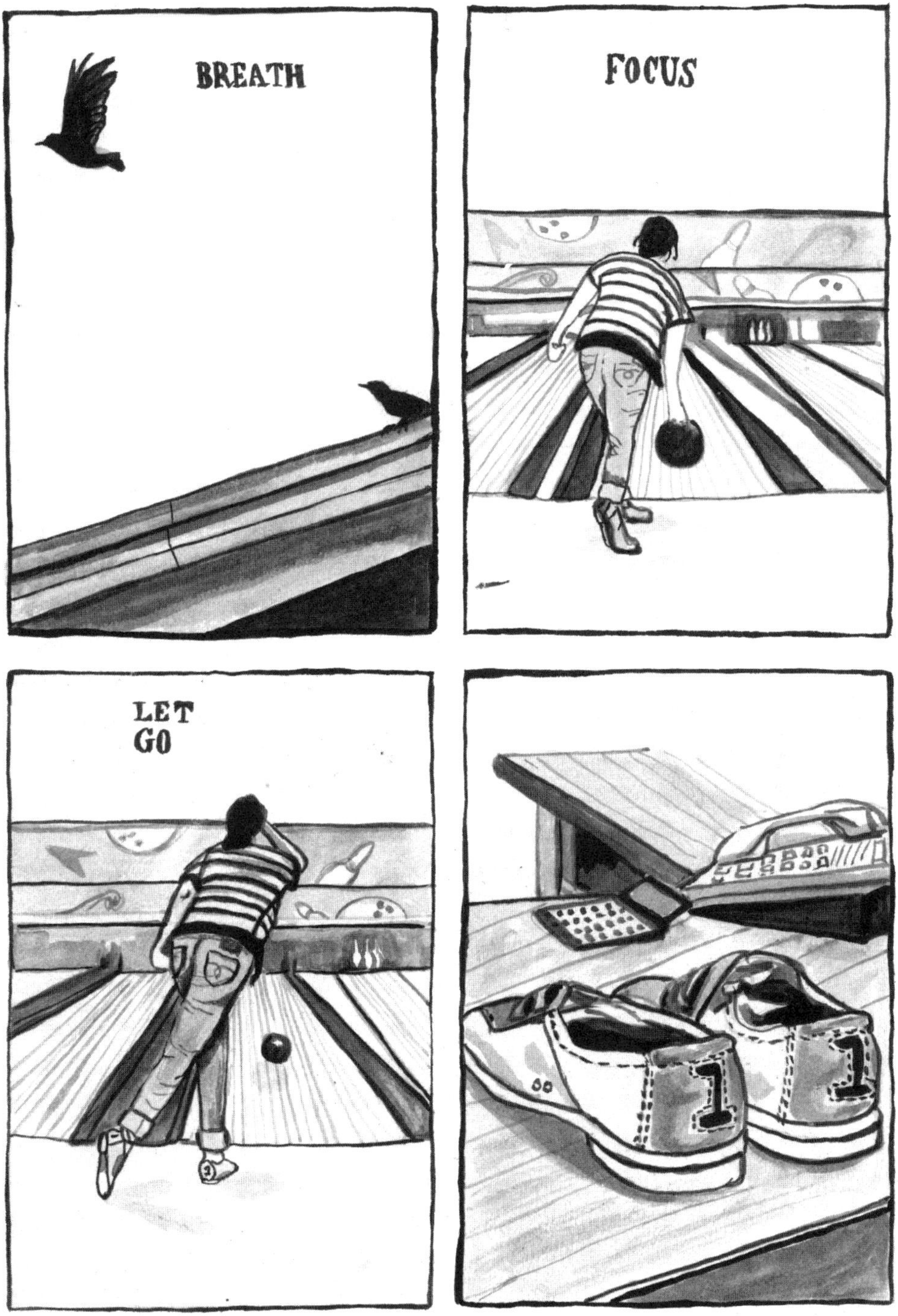
BREATH
FOCUS
LET GO

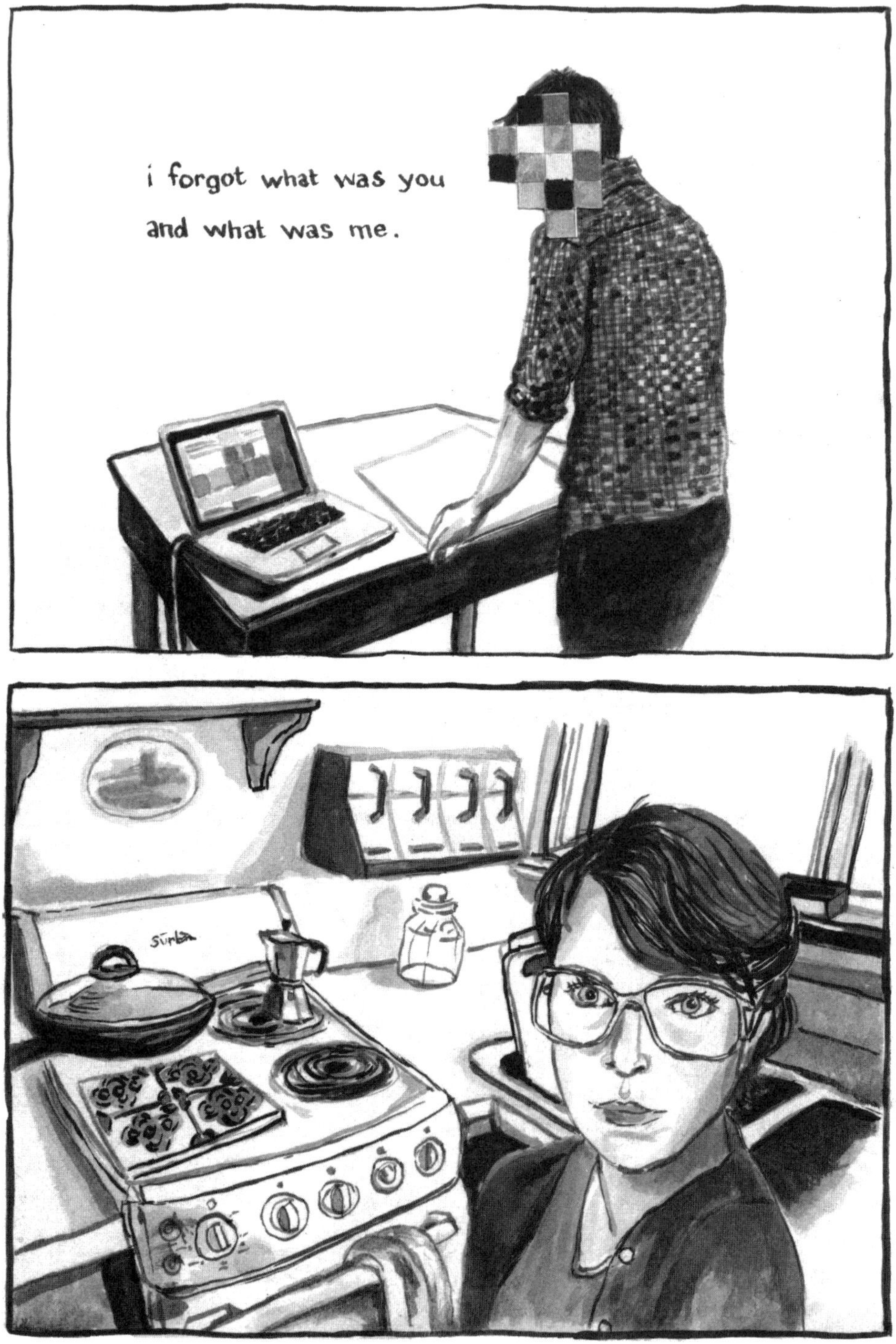
i forgot what was you
and what was me.

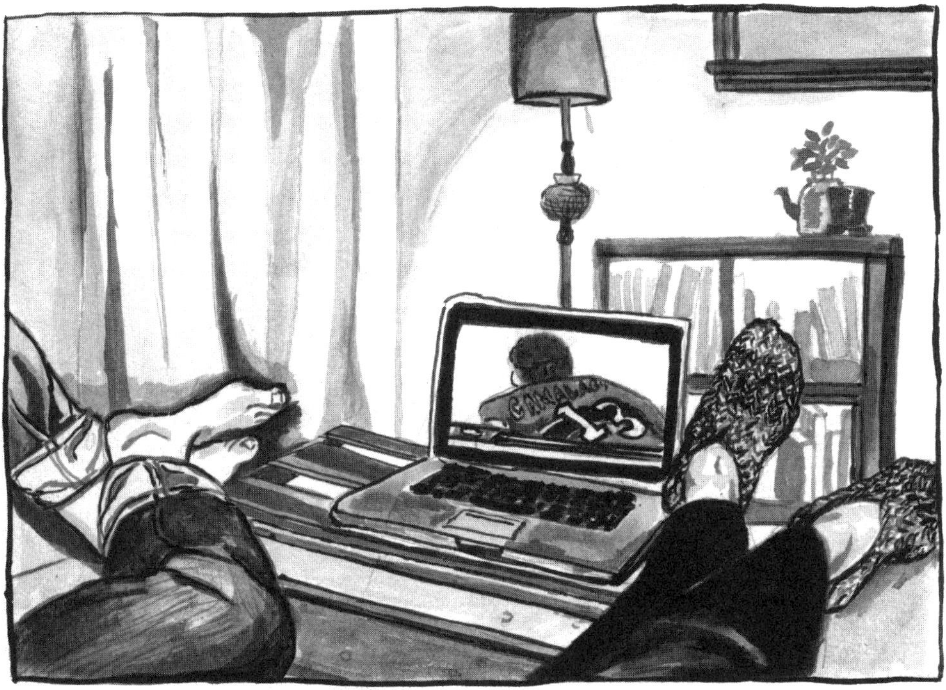

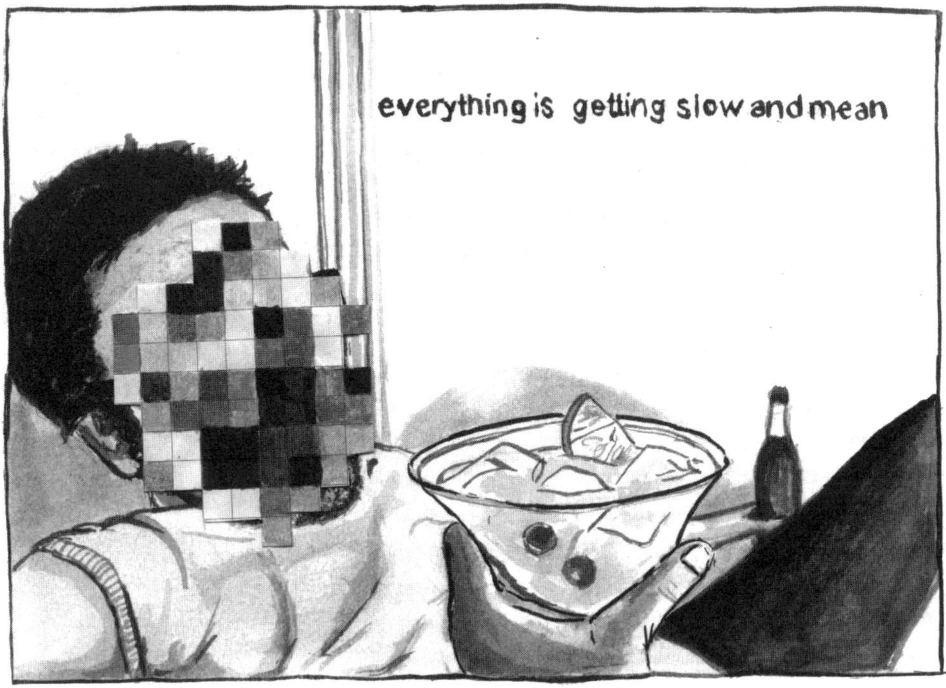
everything is getting slow and mean

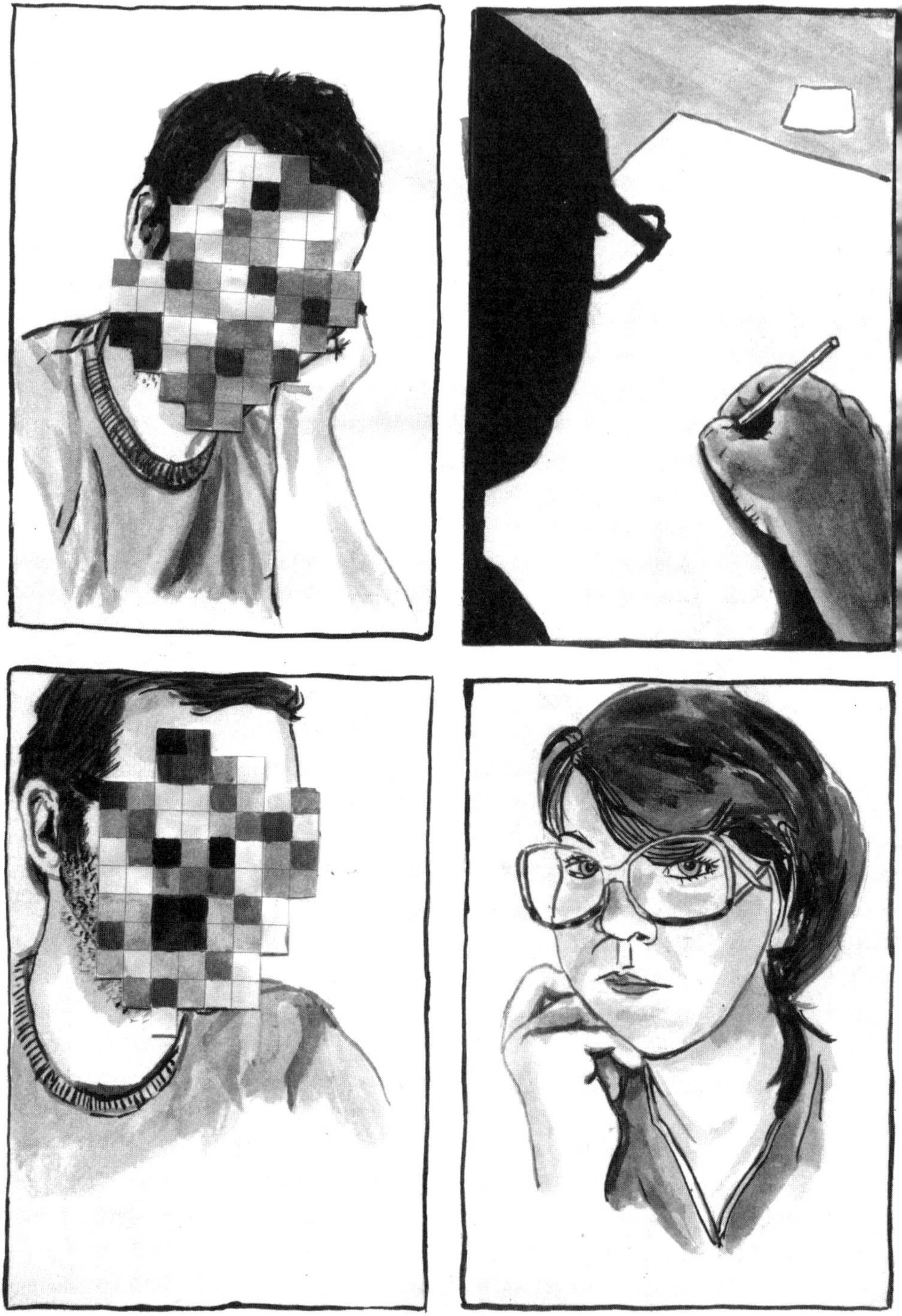

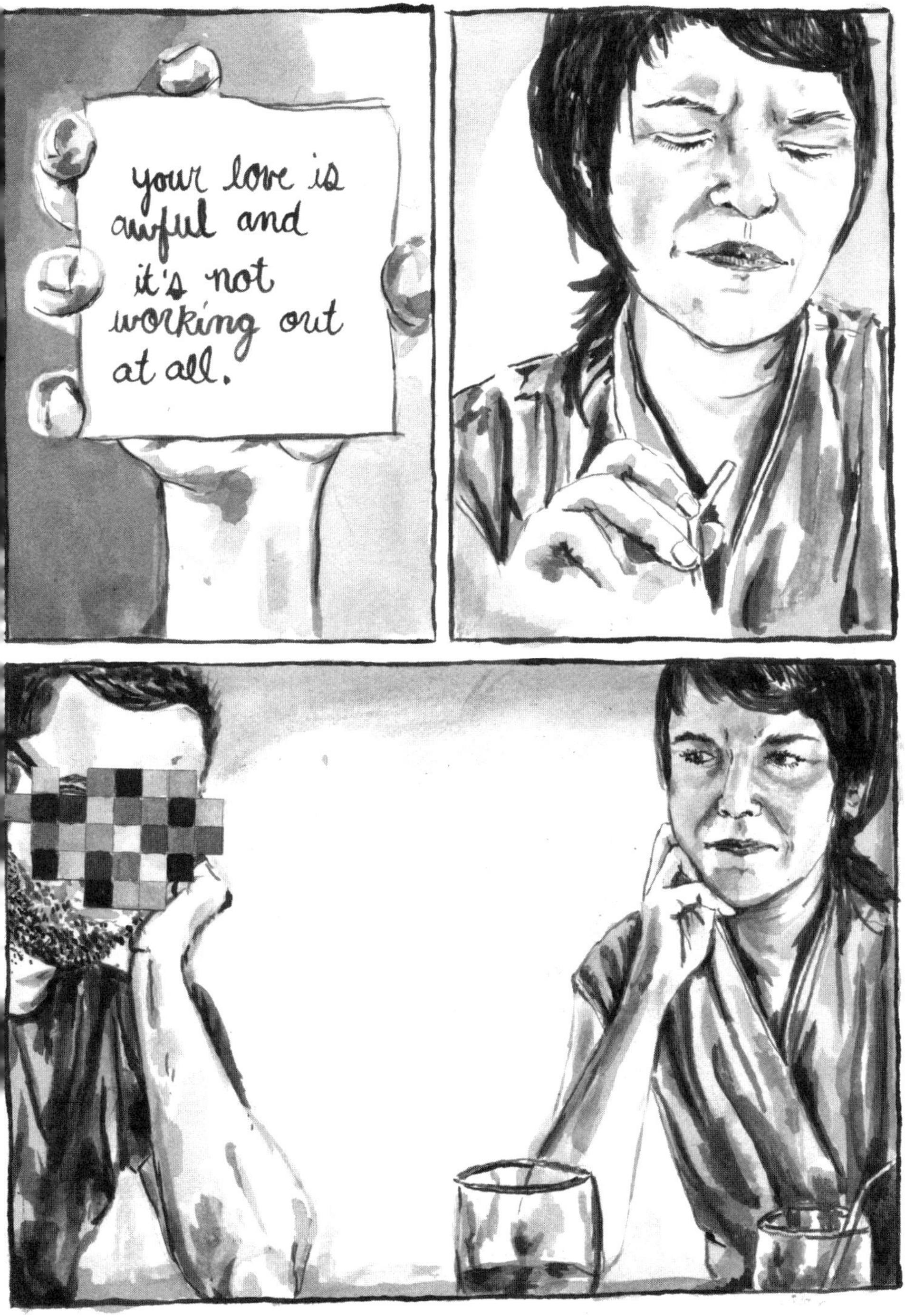
your love is awful and it's not working out at all.

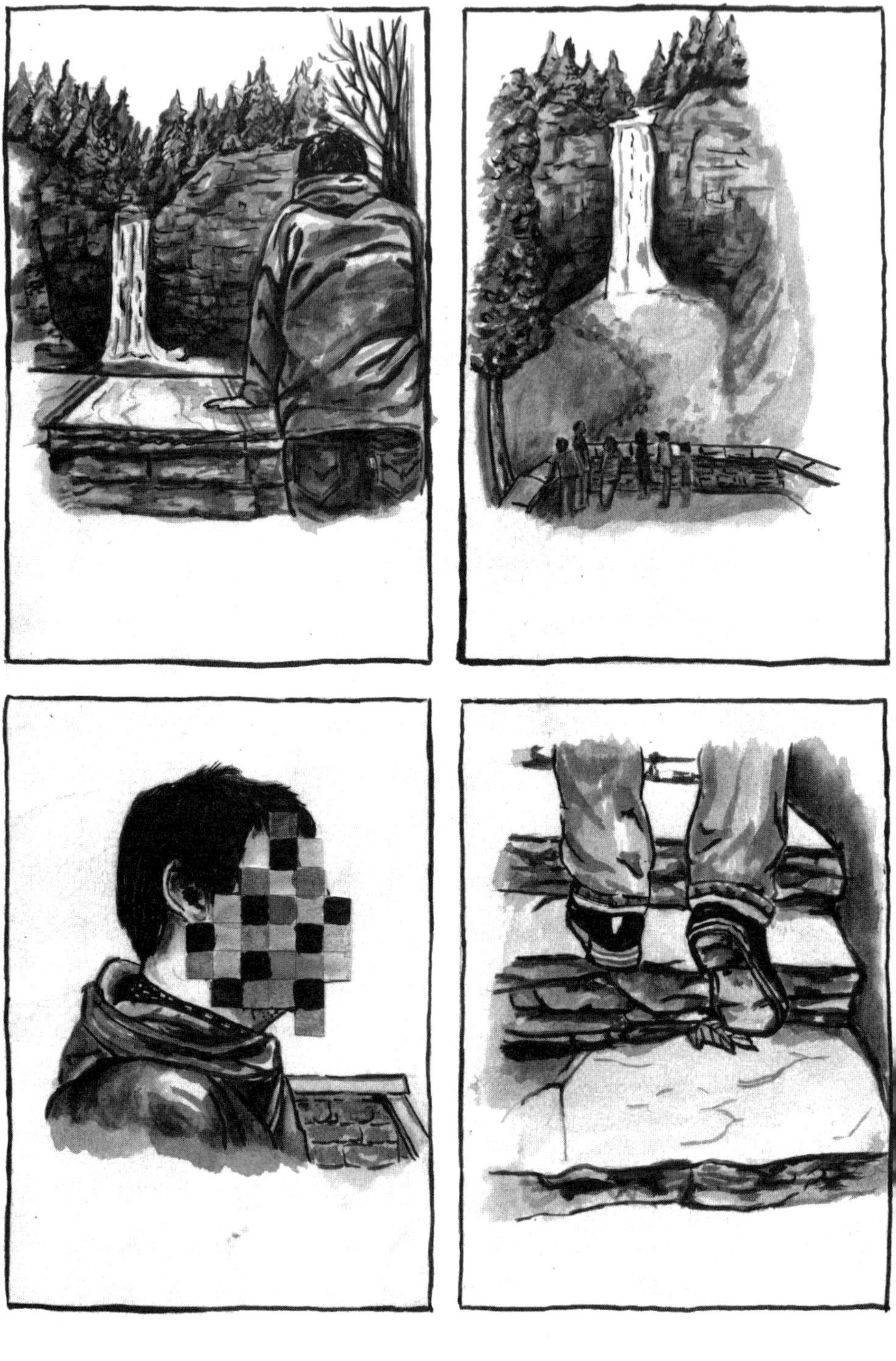

That shitty
ring never fit.
And no matter how many times
I listen to the good karma divorce
self help audio tape while running
myself to death on a treadmill
at that creepy 24 hour gym
I just ~~love~~ hate you.
Like forever.

Still life lesson no.1

drawing negative space

draw only what is around and in between the subject
(the subject is a positive shape)
Squint until the negative space forms shapes
Fill in the empty space, the air, the nothing
That surrounds the positive shape.

Still life lesson no.2

they say
the hardest part of a painting
is knowing when to stop
recognizing when it's done
He doesn't love you and it's okay.

Still life lesson no.3

draw from life
trust your eyes
draw only what you see
not what you think you see.
no tracing
no erasers
no photographs

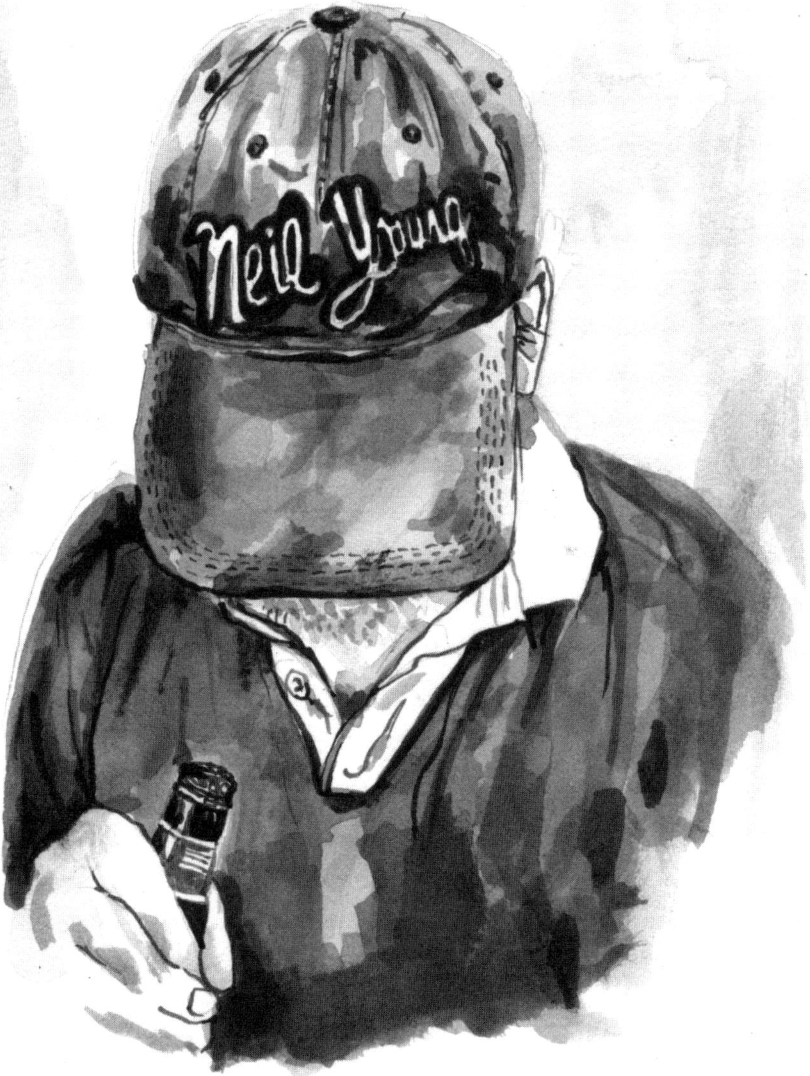
Neil Young

i got a job in northern alberta
i move there on tuesday and
start teaching (drawing)
on wednesday

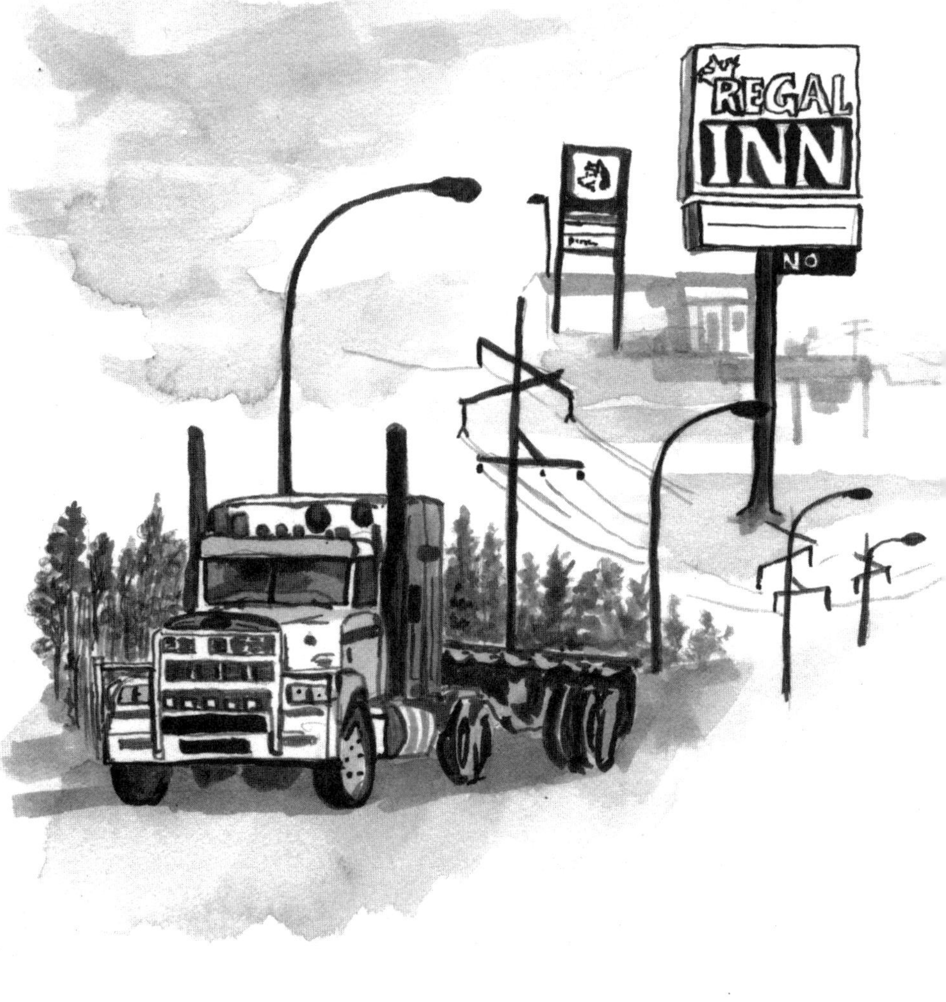
REGAL
INN
NO

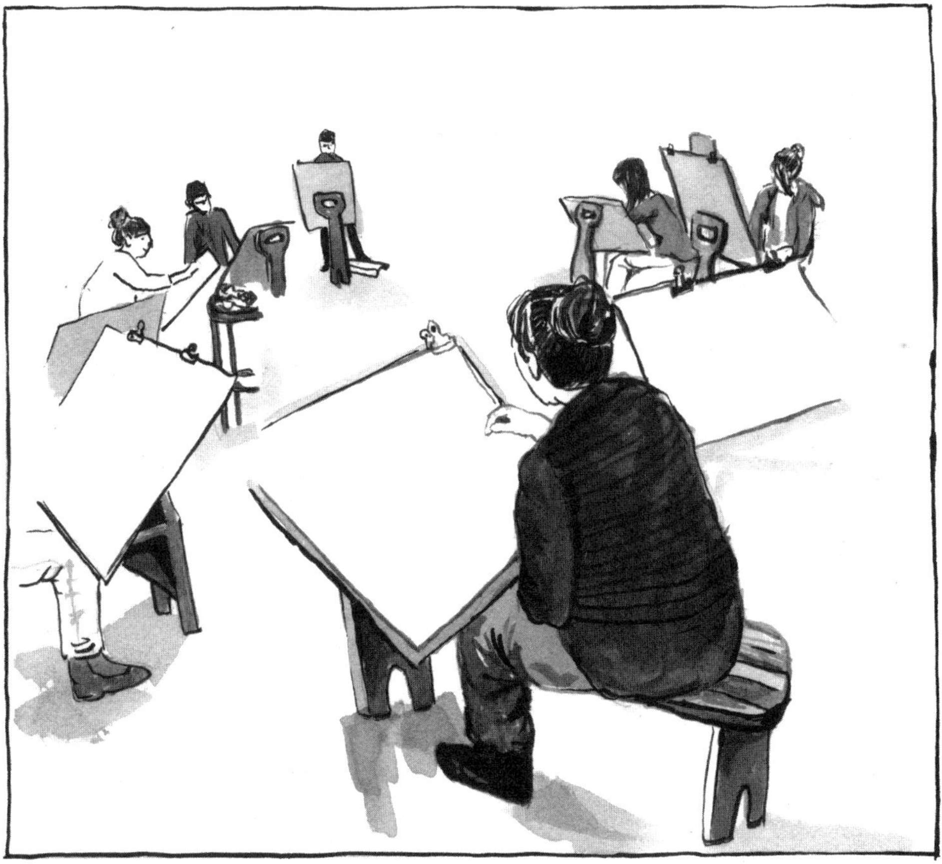

Christmas College Staff Party
Northern Alberta

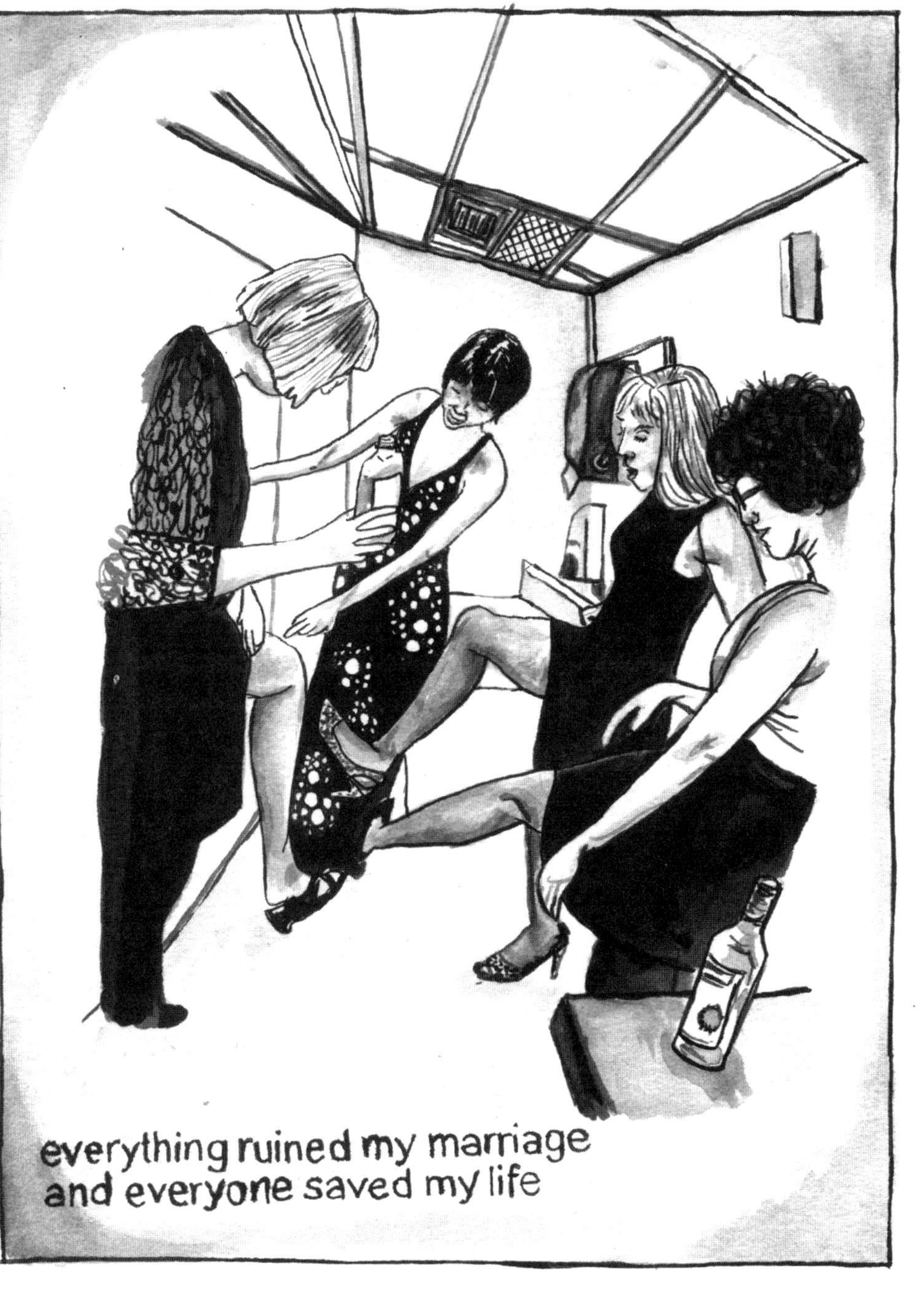
everything ruined my marriage
and everyone saved my life

The seven weapons necessary for the spiritual combat (it's -50°C)

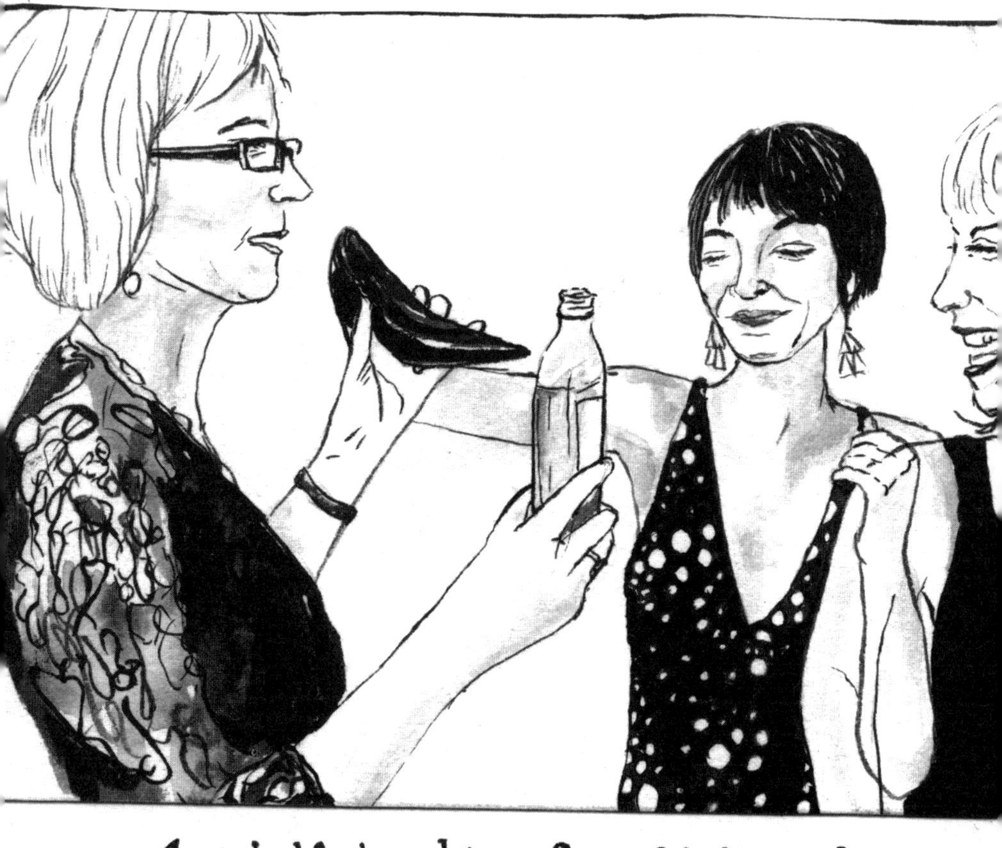

1. girlfriends 2. whiskey shoe

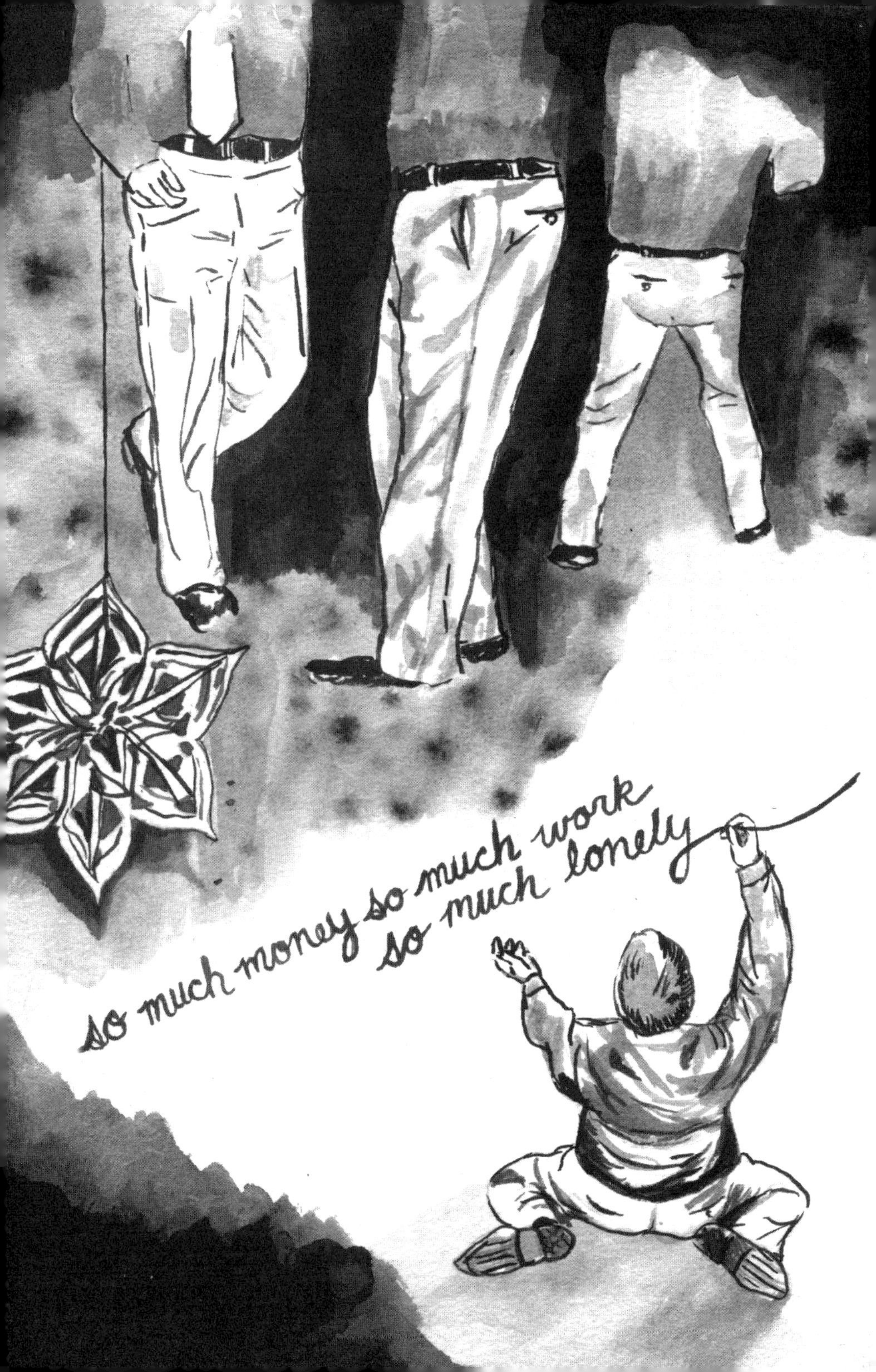
so much money so much work
so much lonely

You are invisible

Go visible
_____ is busy. You may be interrupting

You are running on reserve battery power

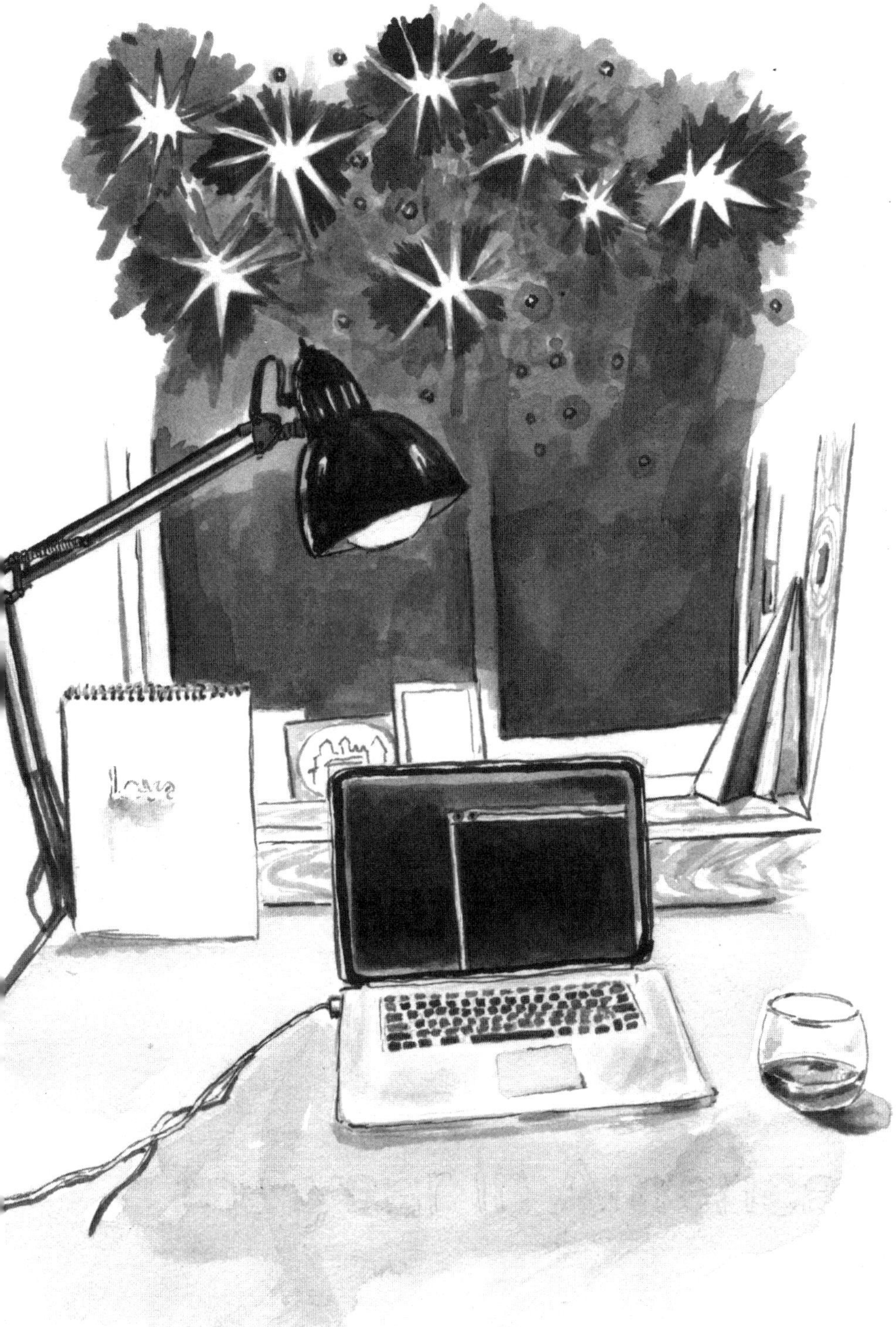

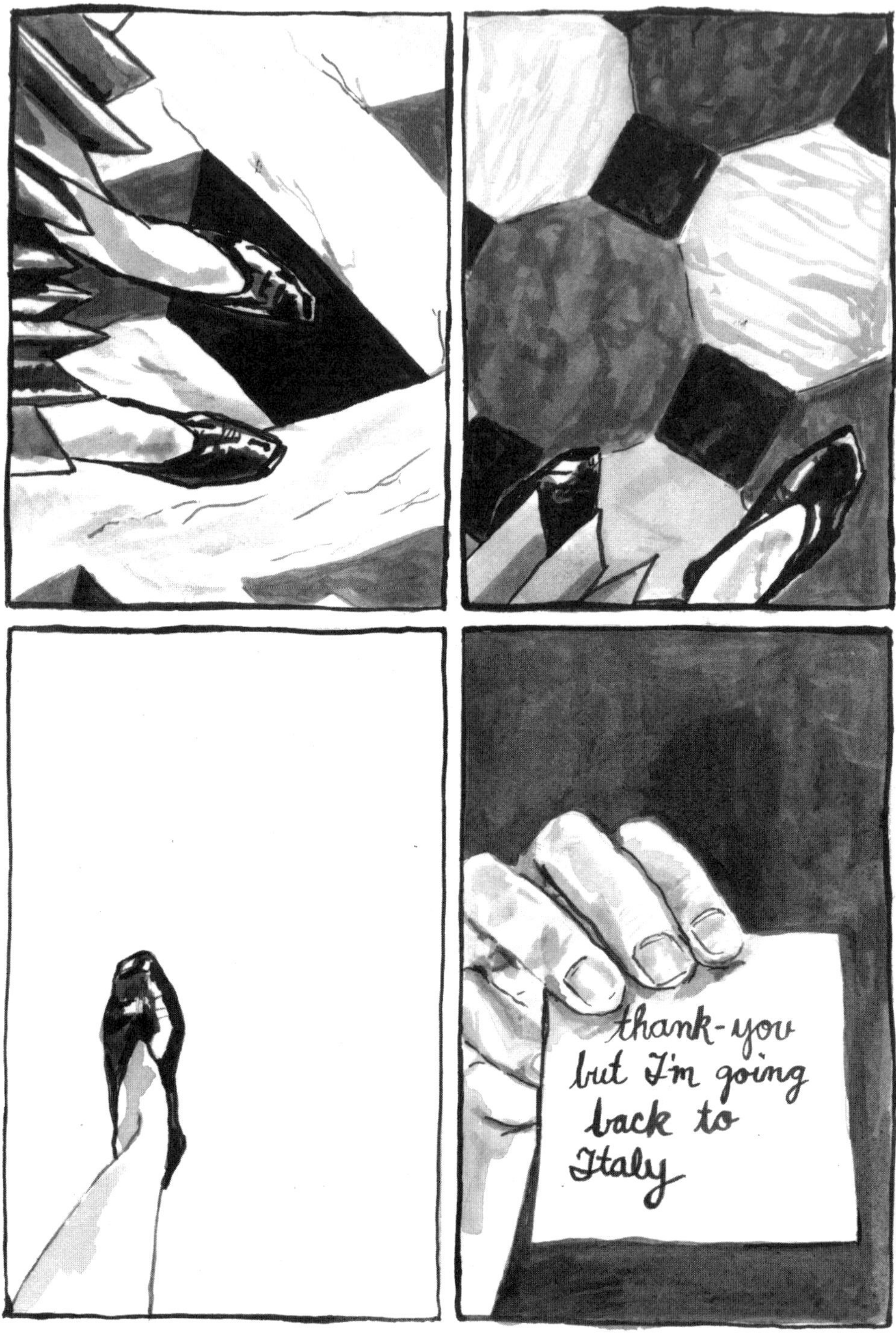
thank-you
but I'm going
back to
Italy

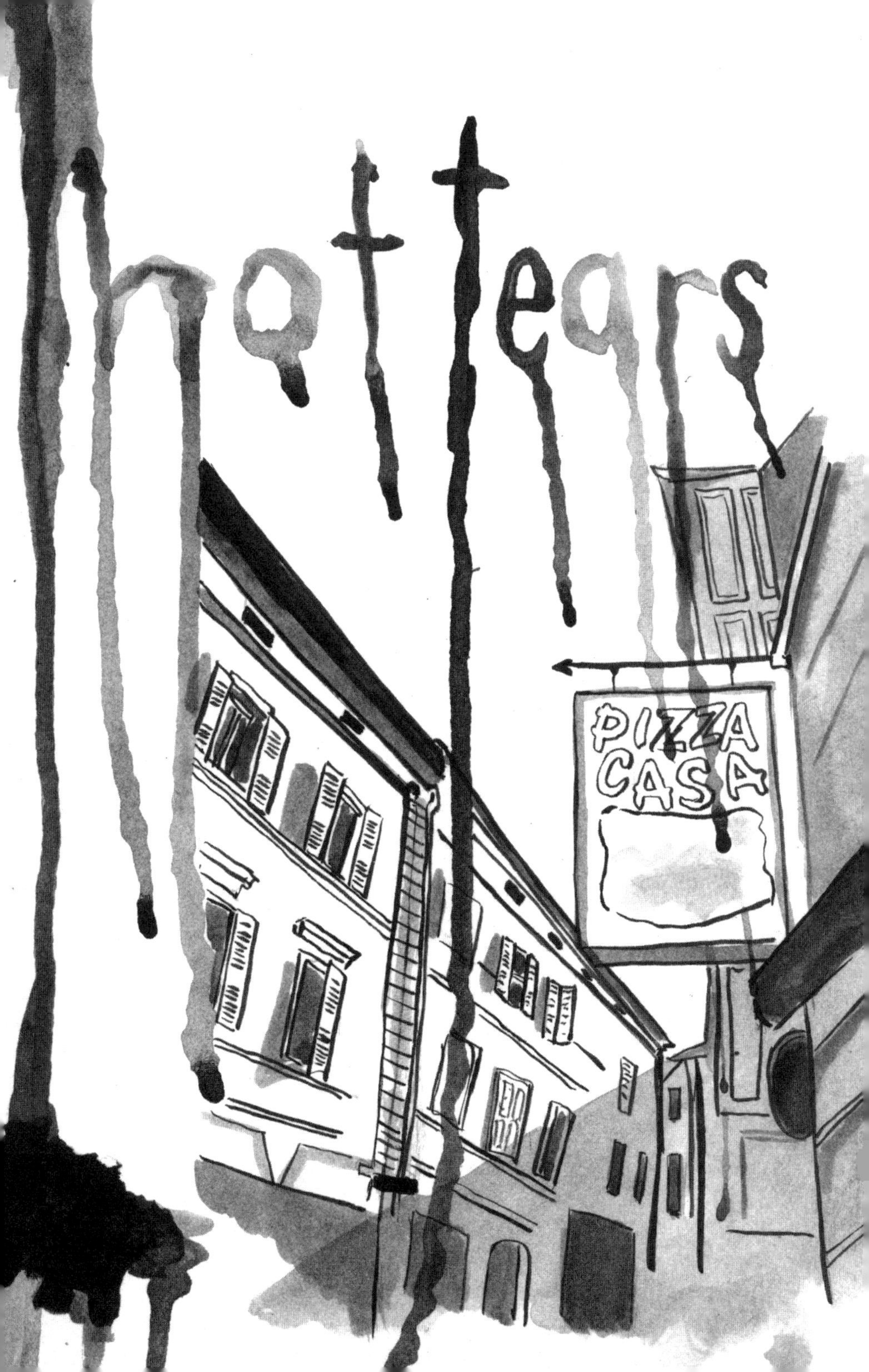
hot tears
PIZZA CASA

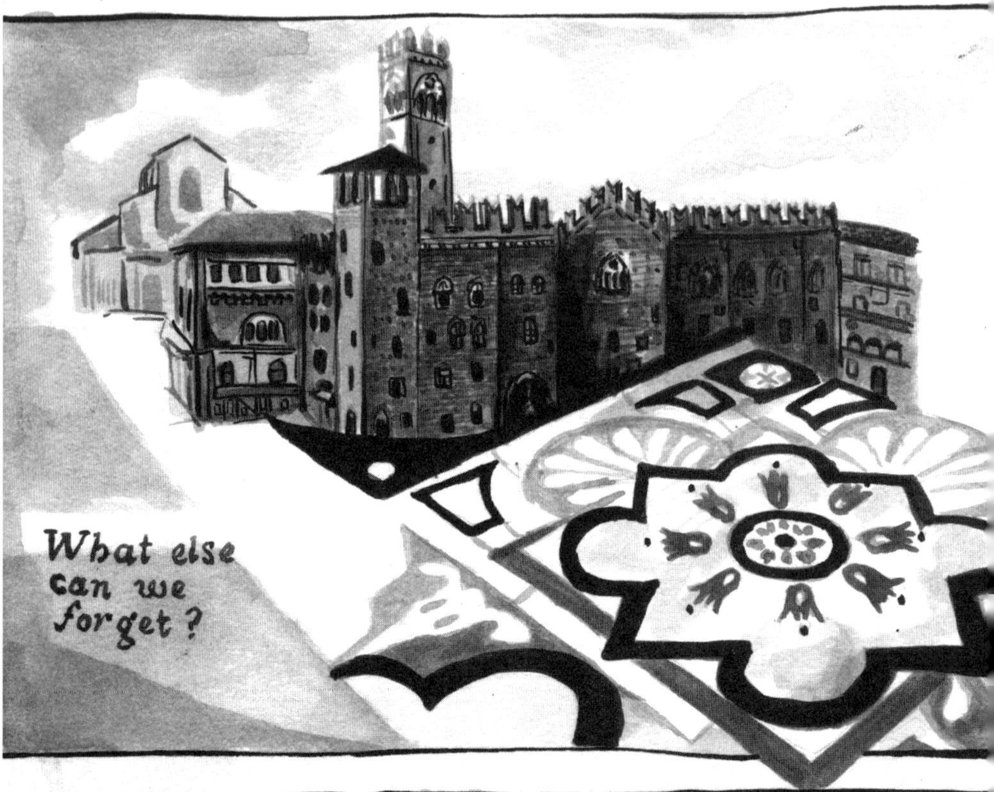
What else can we forget?

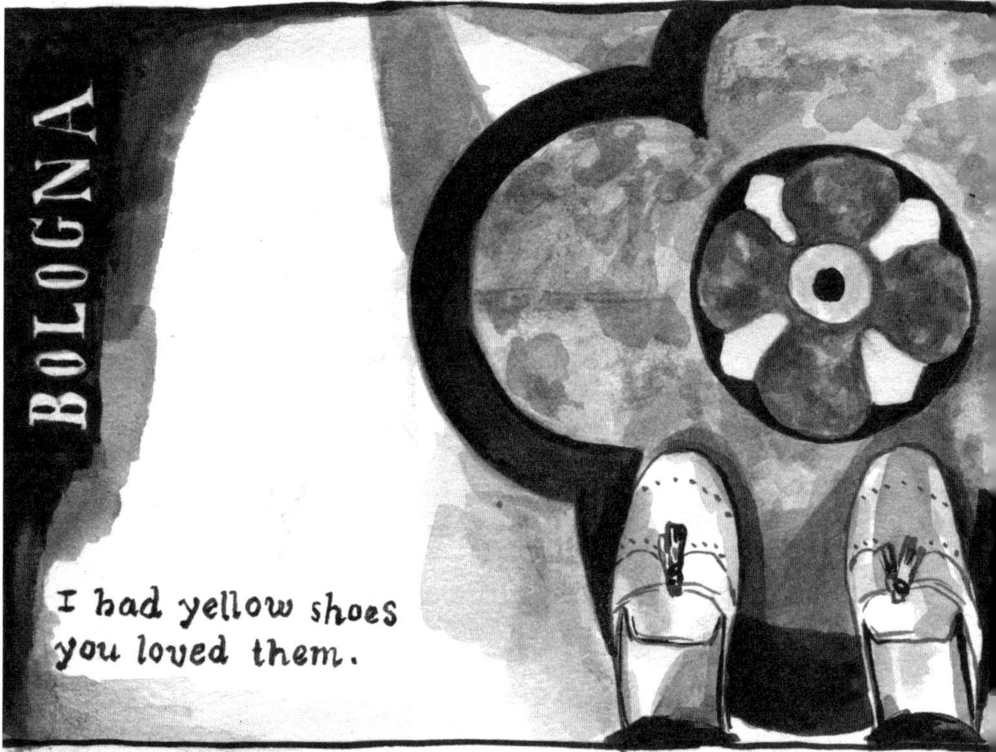
BOLOGNA
I had yellow shoes you loved them.

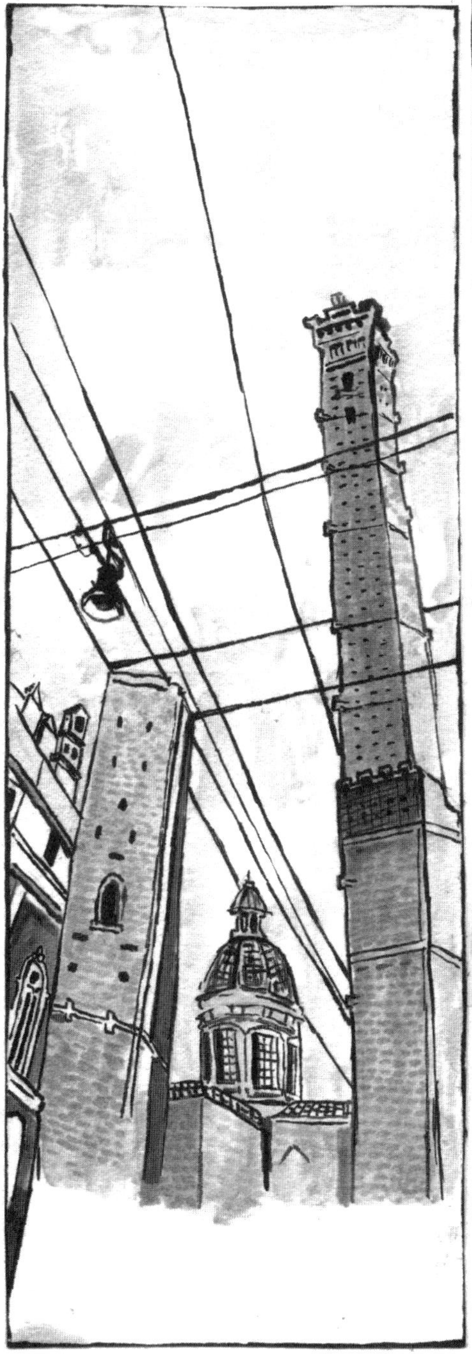
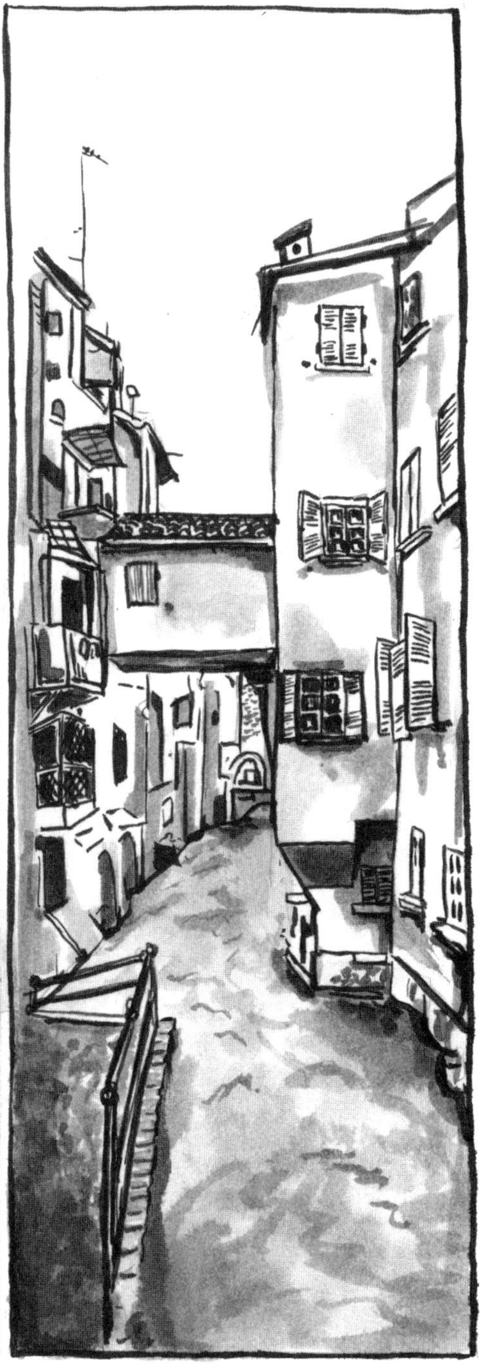

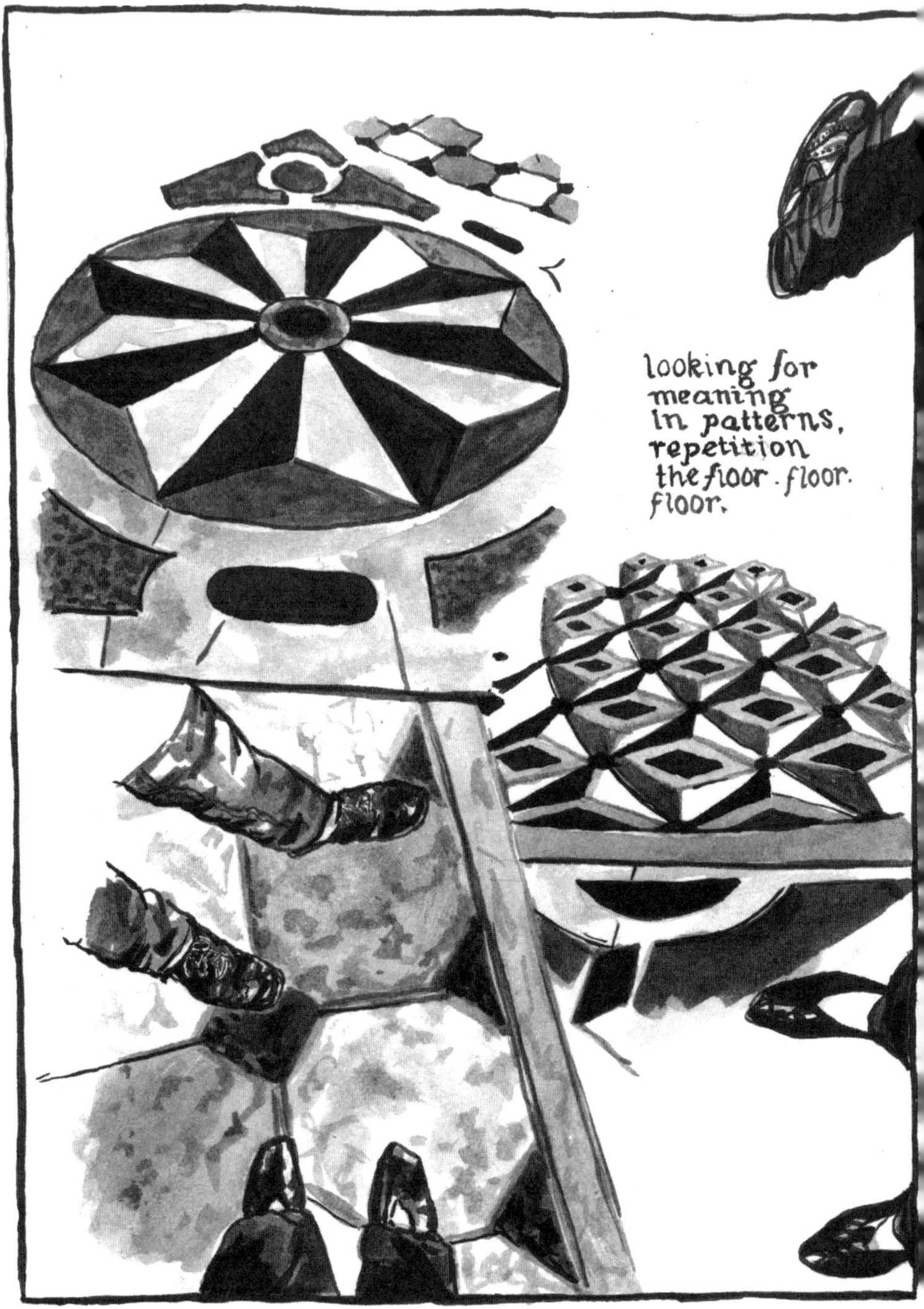
looking for
meaning
in patterns,
repetition
the floor. floor.
floor.

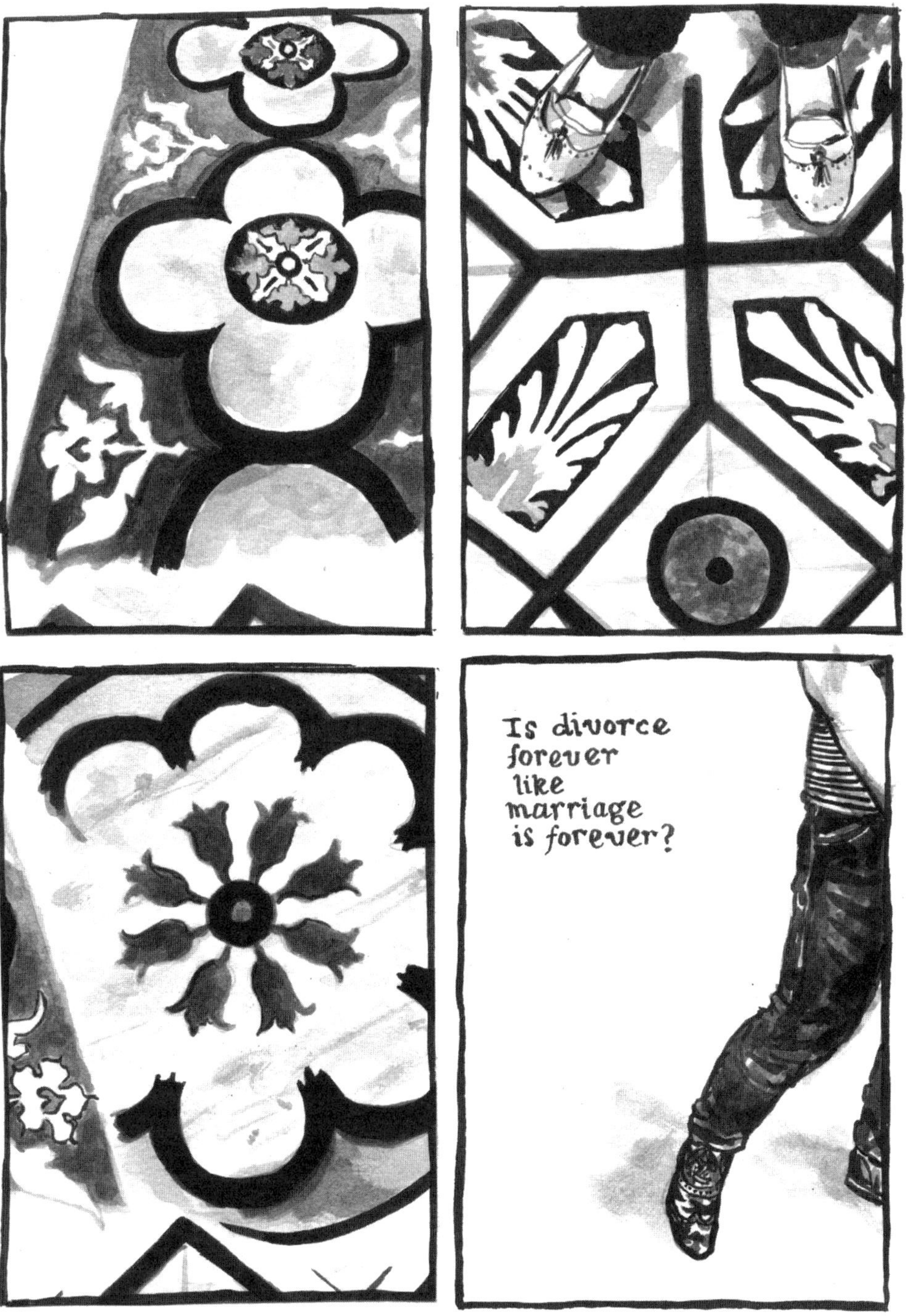
Is divorce forever like marriage is forever?

Terremoto: earthquake

During the earthquake you wait
You wait for someone else
You wait for it to stop
for towers to fall
for birdsongs to return
I watch the plants
because they don't overreact
next time I am going to run.

the pilot said
have a pleasant forward journey

L.hi sister~ am i still allowed to meet you in Paris?

E.YES! see you soon you fancy Euro bean.
E. Love u missy party face + I'm boarding for London now , see you soon !

L. love ya sister!! have a happy flight

E. I couldn't get my India visa on time so I will be in Paris from the 19 th until June 1 st ! So meet me anytime ! Stay as long as you can !

E. Hi missy I'm so tired I could puke so let's Skype mother
L. see you on the 23rd sister! 8:10am lolololol i'll cab or something to wherever you are so you dont have to wake up because thats early as fackk
I'M GOING TO PARIS TO SEE MY SISTER WHAT IS MY LIFE ABOUT

E. oh and wear practical shoes ~ the roads are bumpy and we might have to walk a lot.

L. I don't even care about the mona lisa honestly~ but if you want to see her again we can go. I hear she's pretty underwhelming. I mostly want to eat a lot and check out cool shops. get a picture with the eiffel tower (duh). I don't really care about art museums but if you really want to check them out I can try to get into it. I wouldn't mind checking out the louvre and palace of versailles. (are those things even in Paris??) and only if they don't cost a ton of money. I usually wake up and wing it most days~ and that makes me happy.
oh yeah! and what is the deal with bringing makeup on planes??

1 ETAGE
- don't laugh at nudity
- learn art history (again)

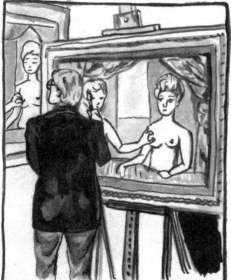

Here Gabrielle d'Estrées sister pinches her nipple to announce that she is pregnant (King Henry IV is the dad fancy)

Gabrielle is the Kings mistress - and I don't know how this is

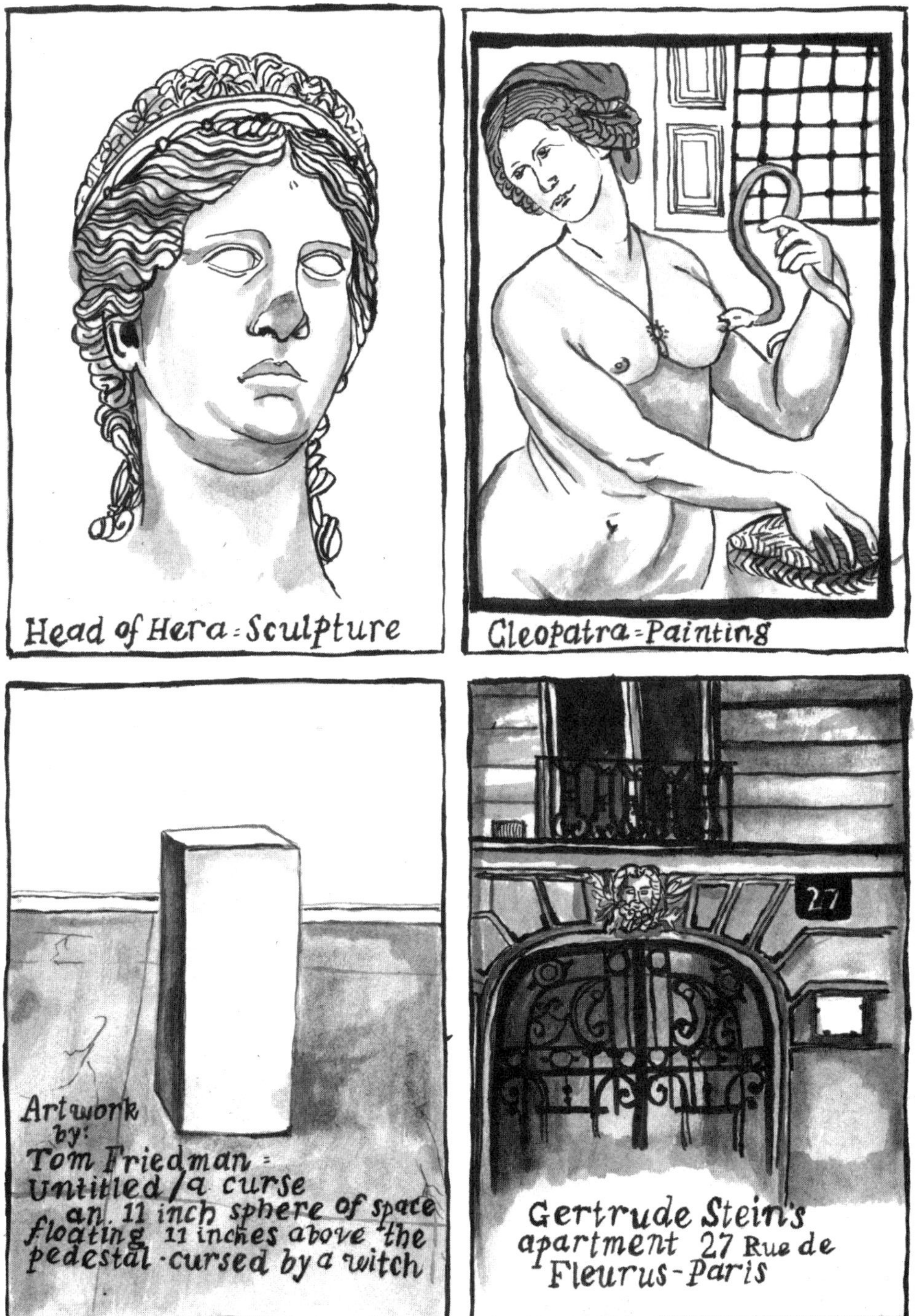
Head of Hera = Sculpture
Cleopatra = Painting
Artwork by: Tom Friedman = Untitled / a curse an 11 inch sphere of space floating 11 inches above the pedestal - cursed by a witch
27
Gertrude Stein's apartment 27 Rue de Fleurus - Paris

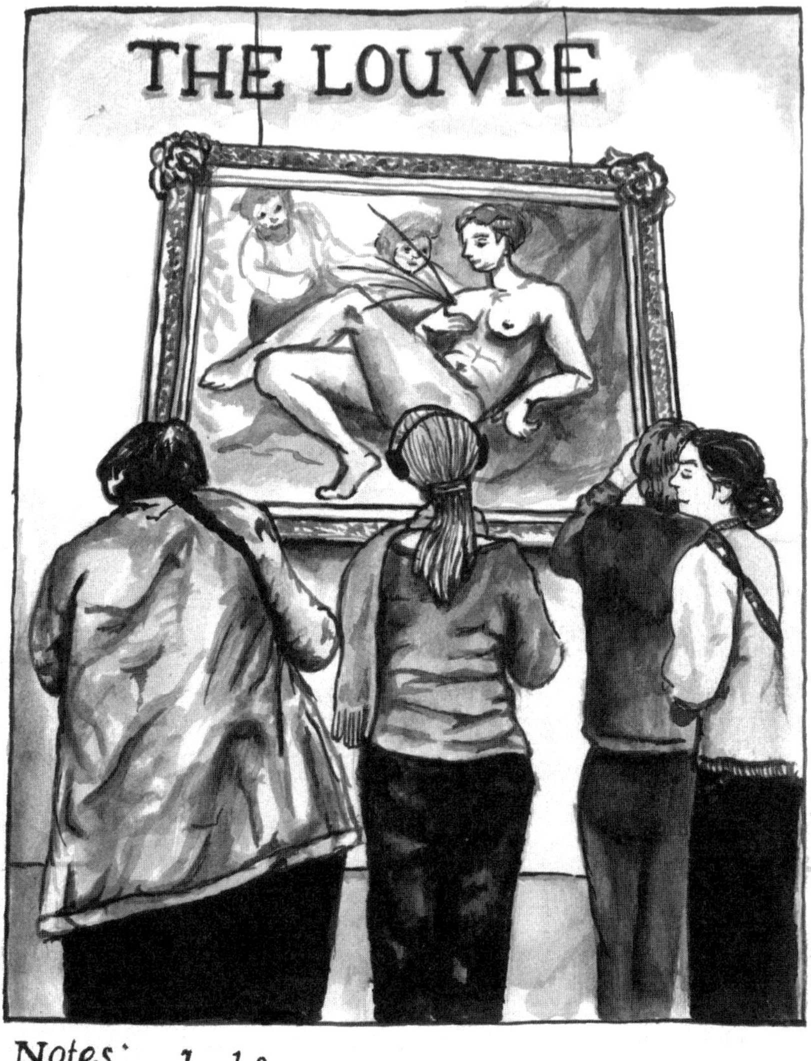
THE LOUVRE

Notes: *boobs*

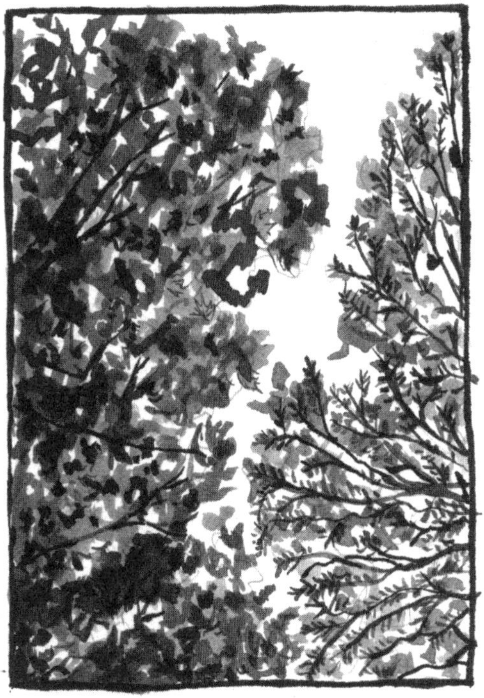

tree tops over
Gertrude Stein

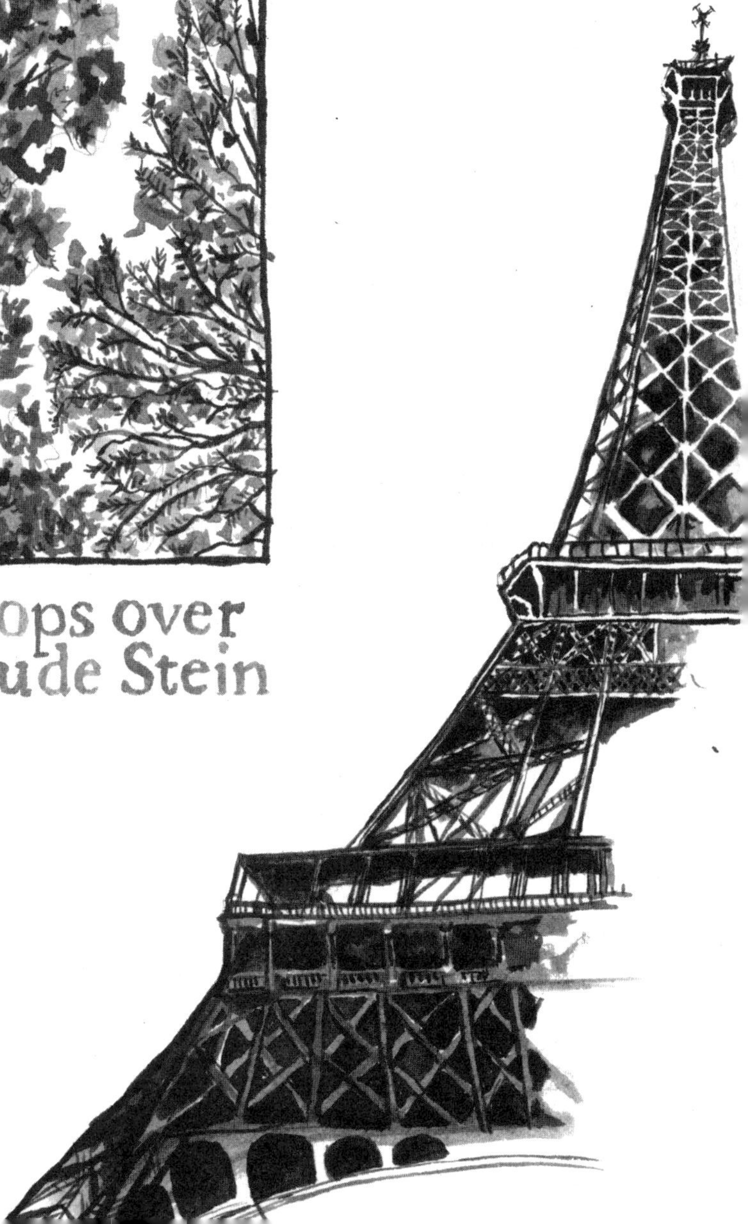

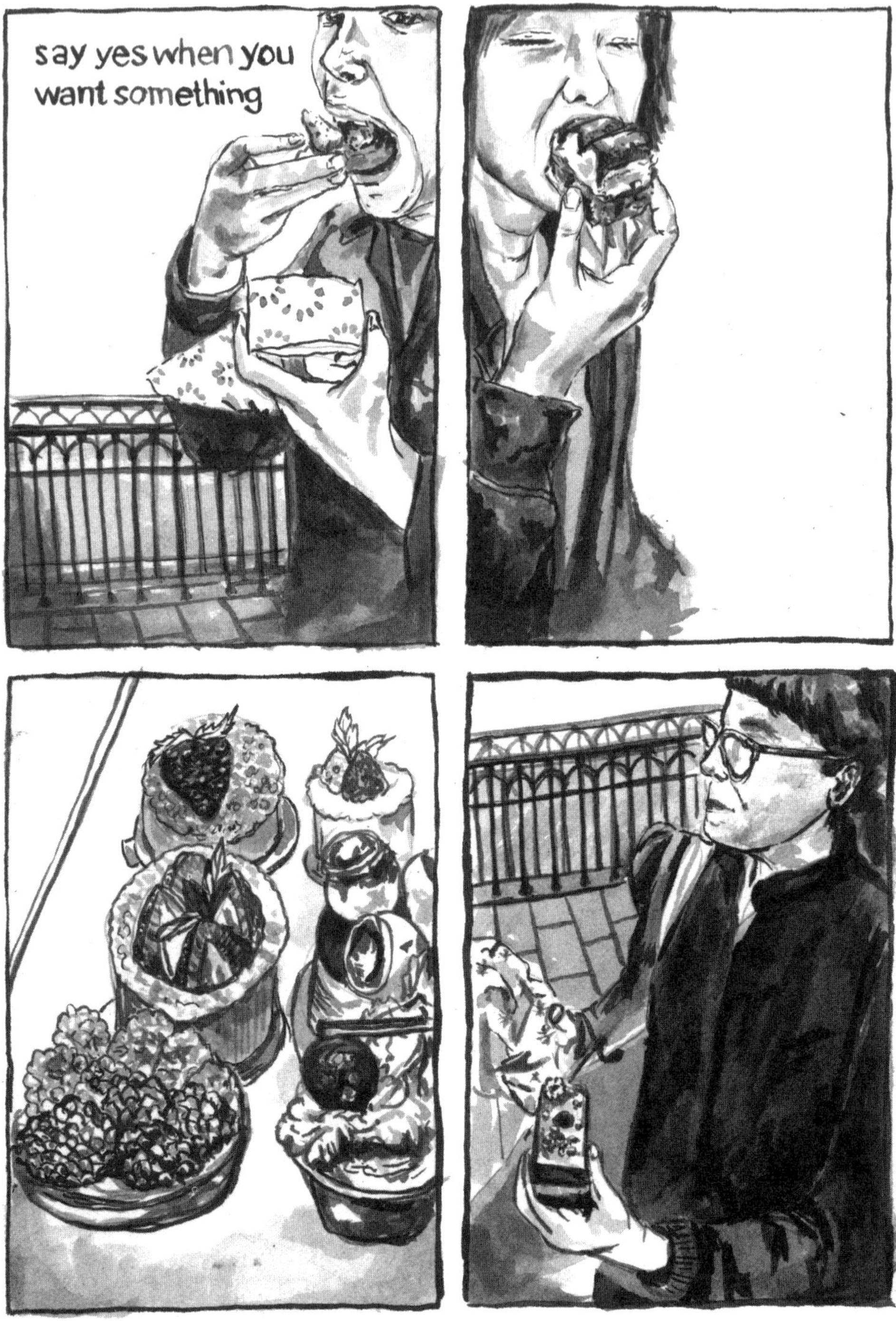
say yes when you want something

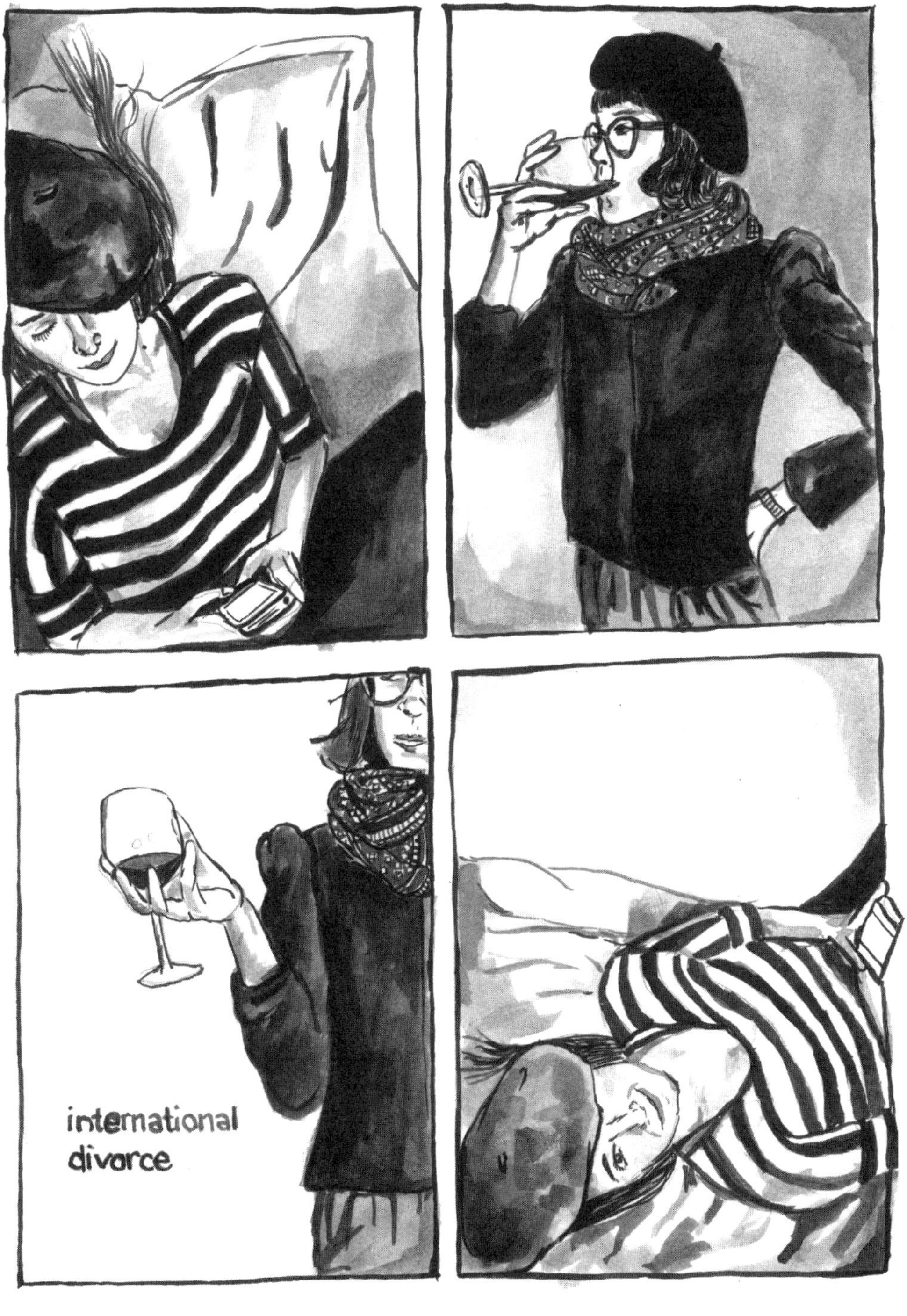
international
divorce

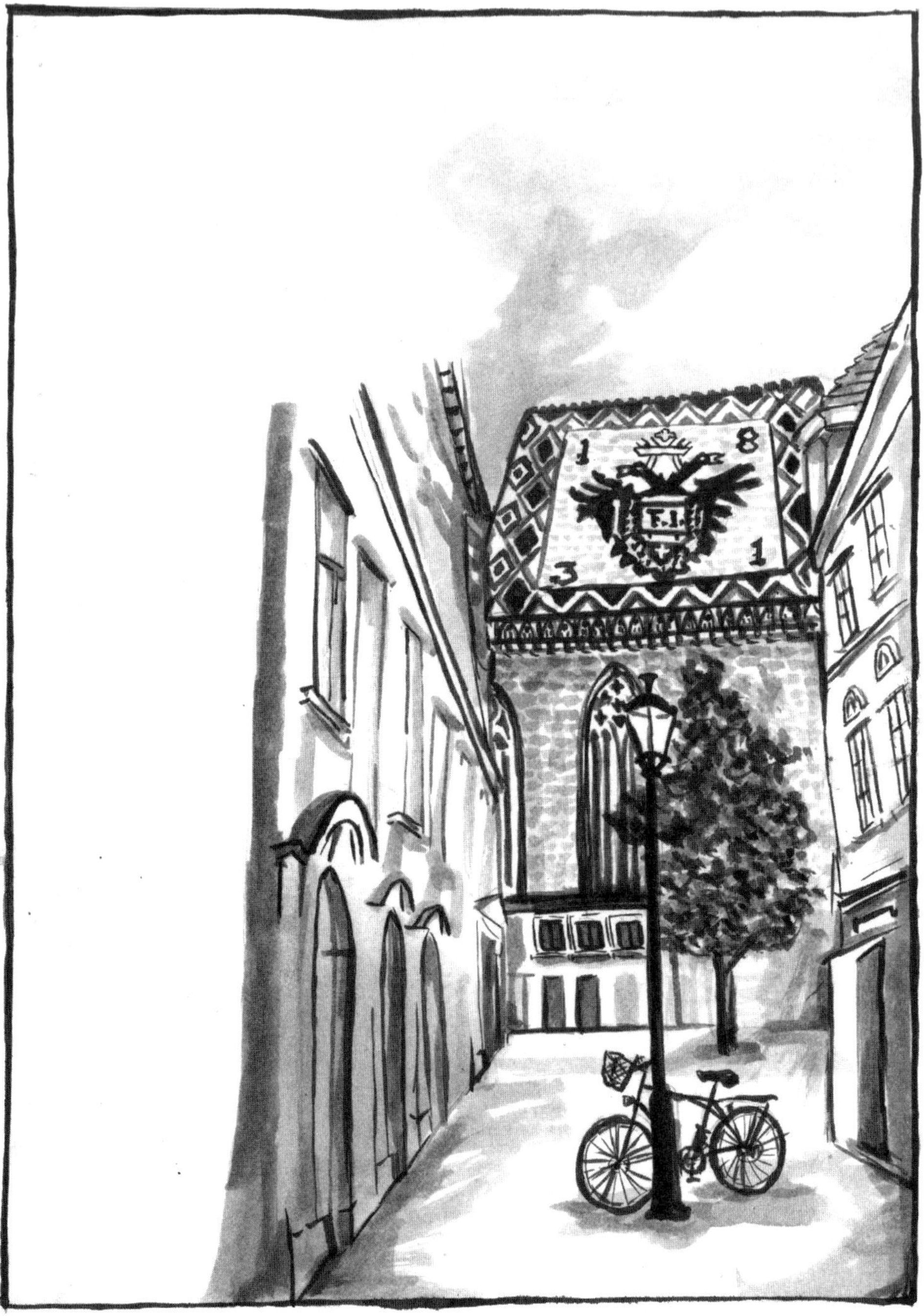
1
8
F.I.
3
1

my little sister: an aupere in Austria

excellent solution to avoid paying student loans:
go babysit four little girls in another country
live in the world
go.

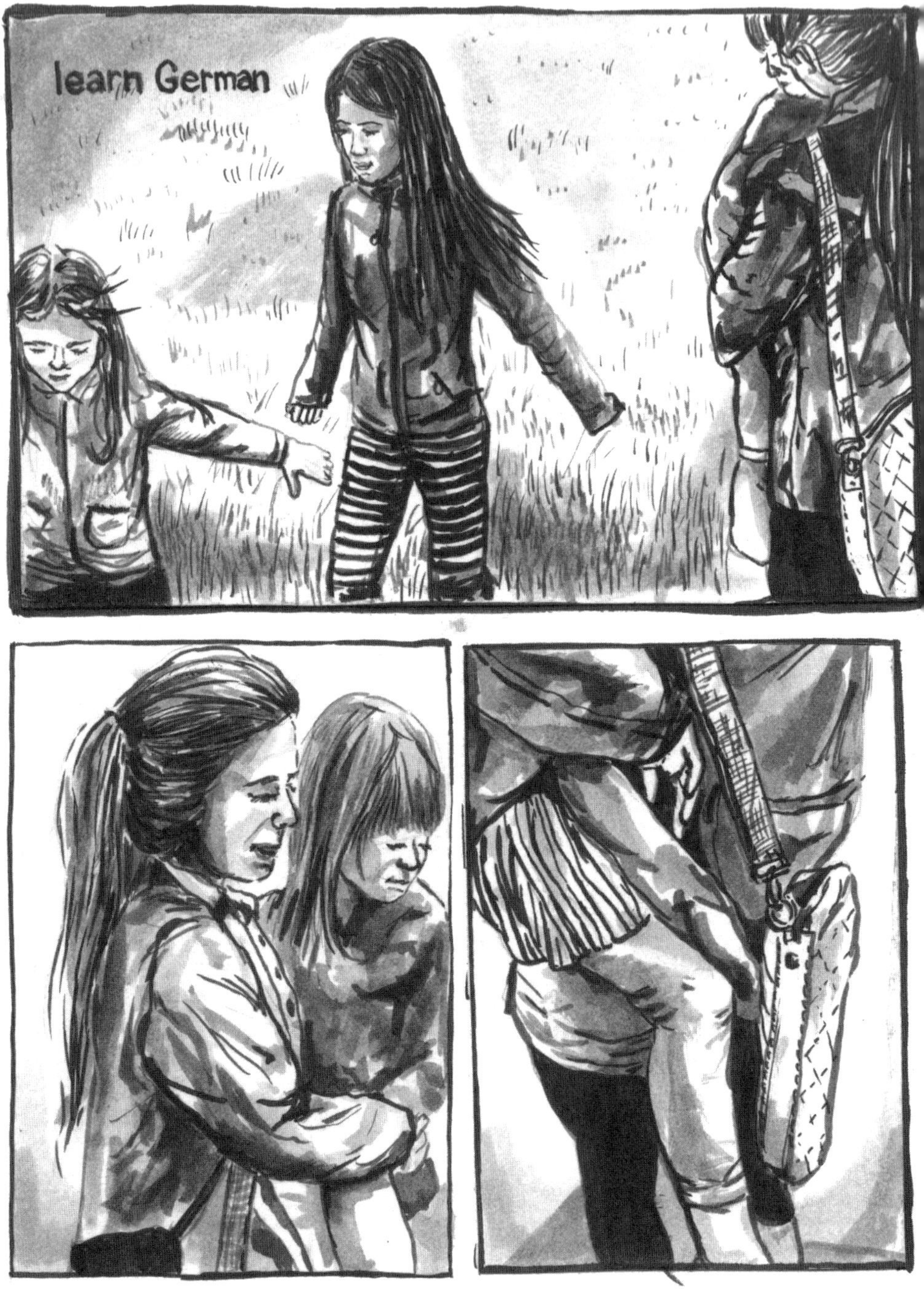
learn German

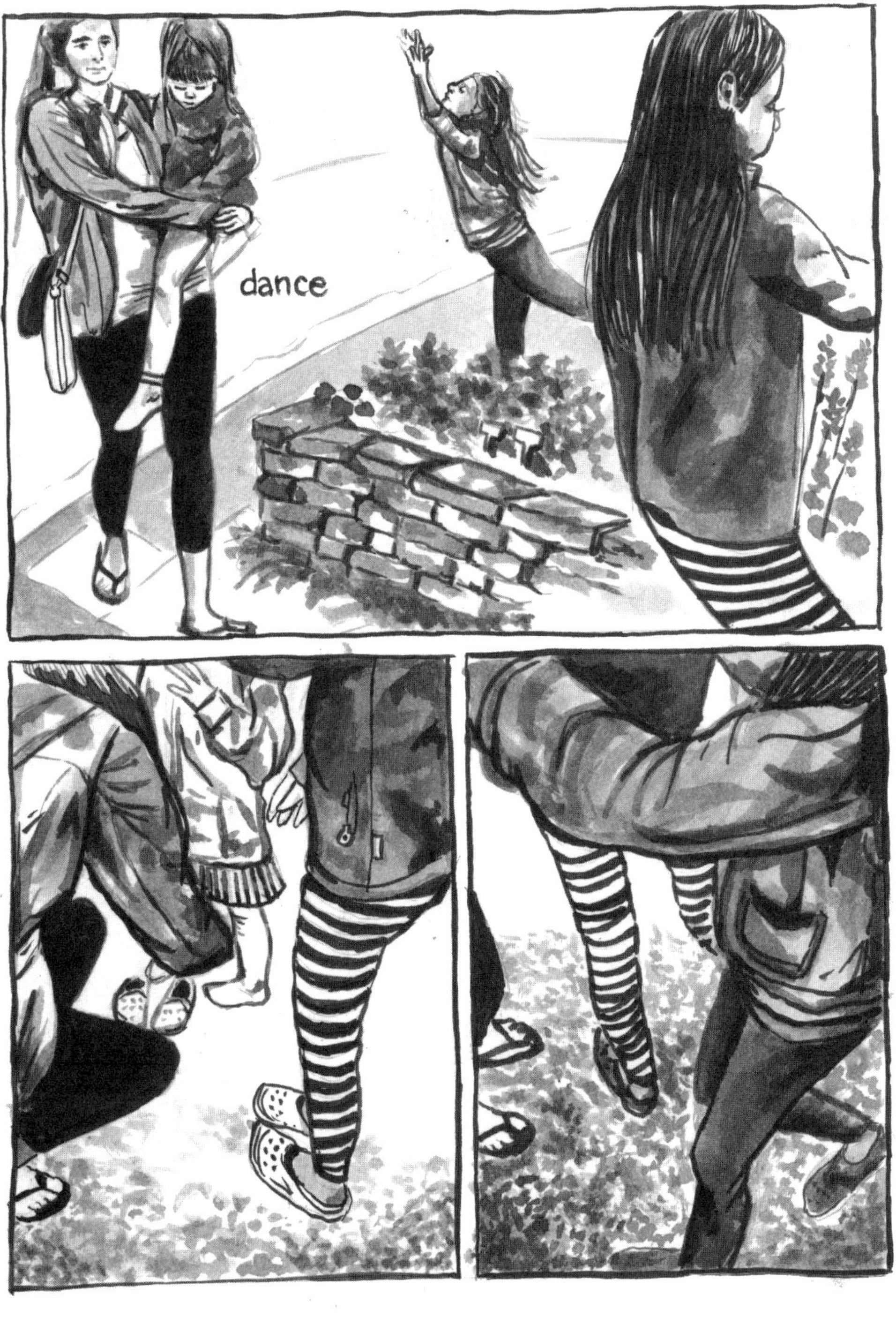
dance

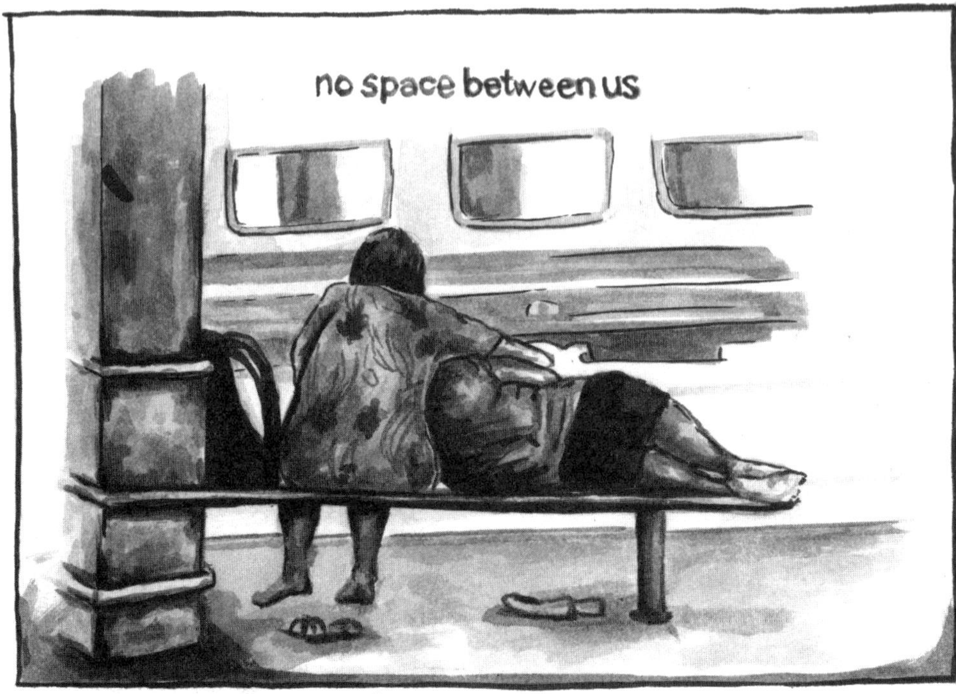
no space between us

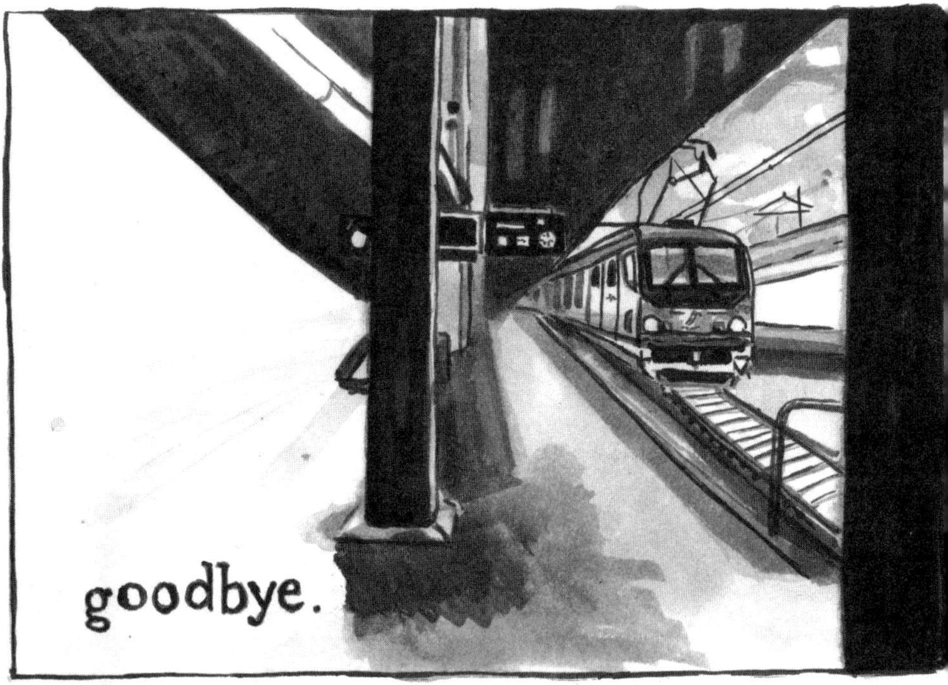
goodbye.

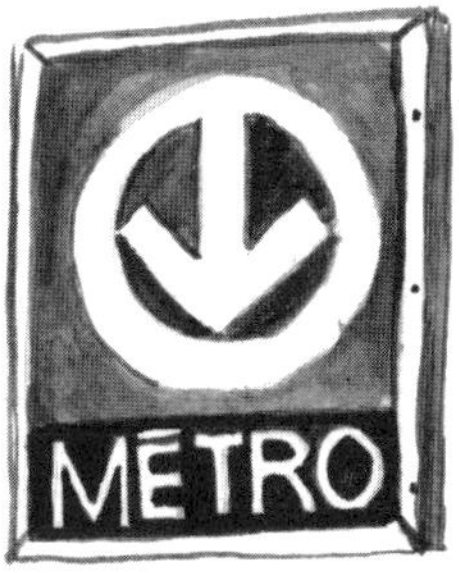
MÉTRO

Montréal part deux

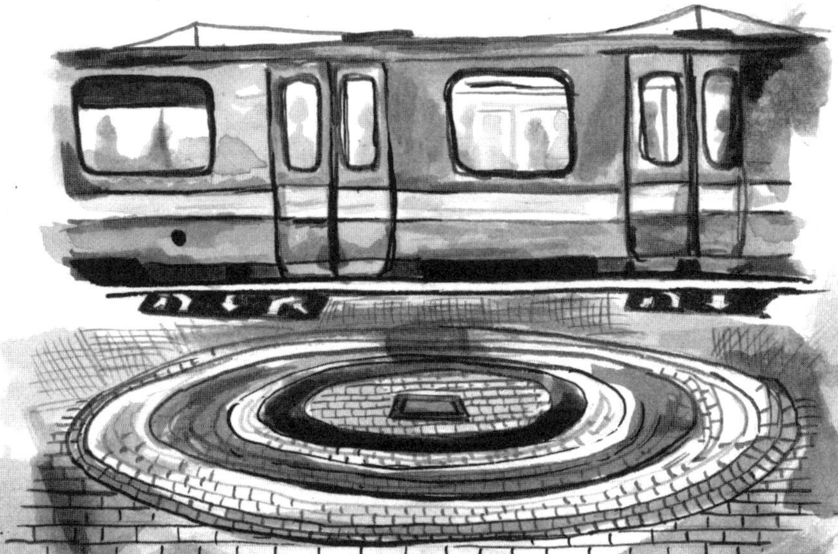

learning not to go away
from her(e)

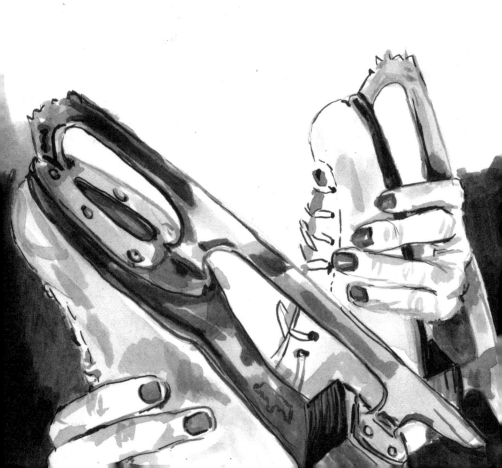

notes for a **new good** future:
- keep your friends
- get old
- get fancy
- risk more sea crossings

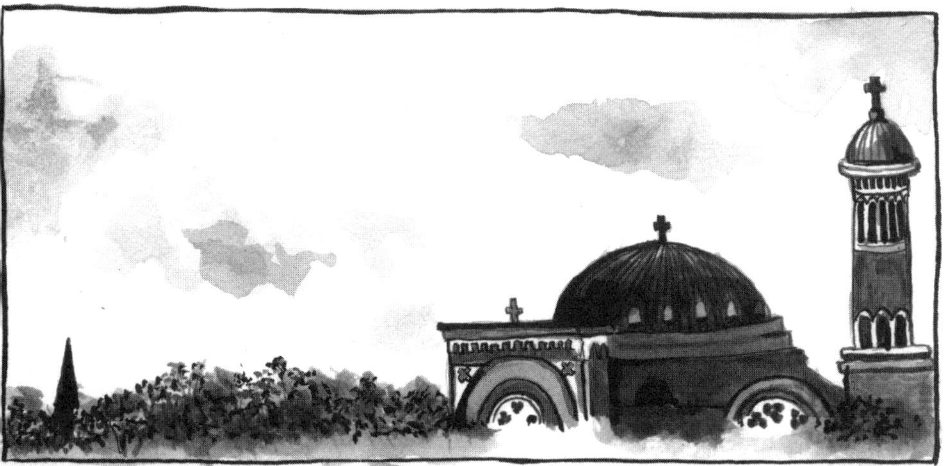

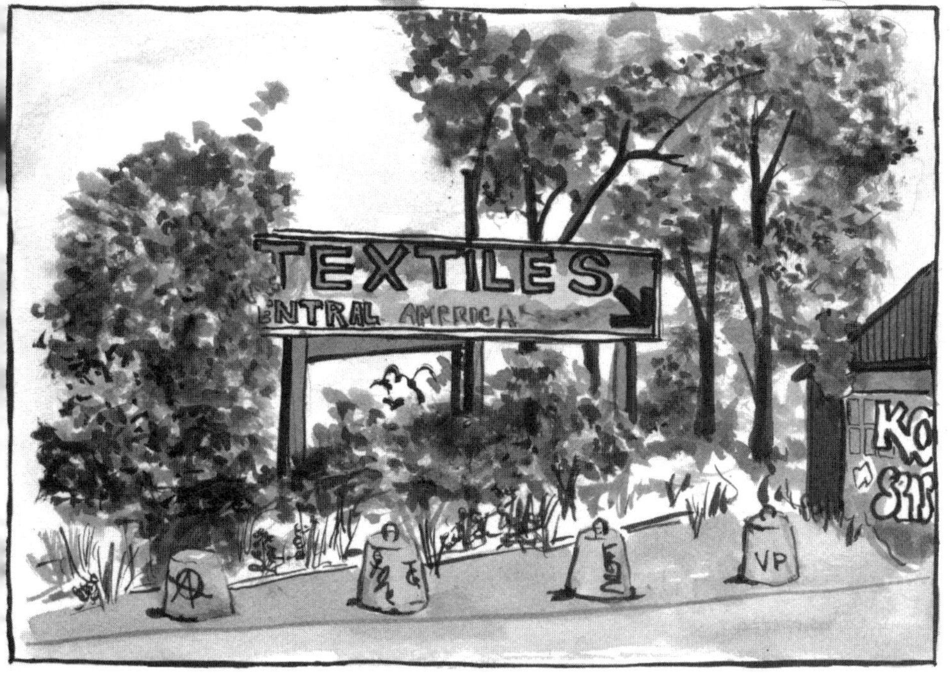
TEXTILES
ENTRAL AMERICA
VP

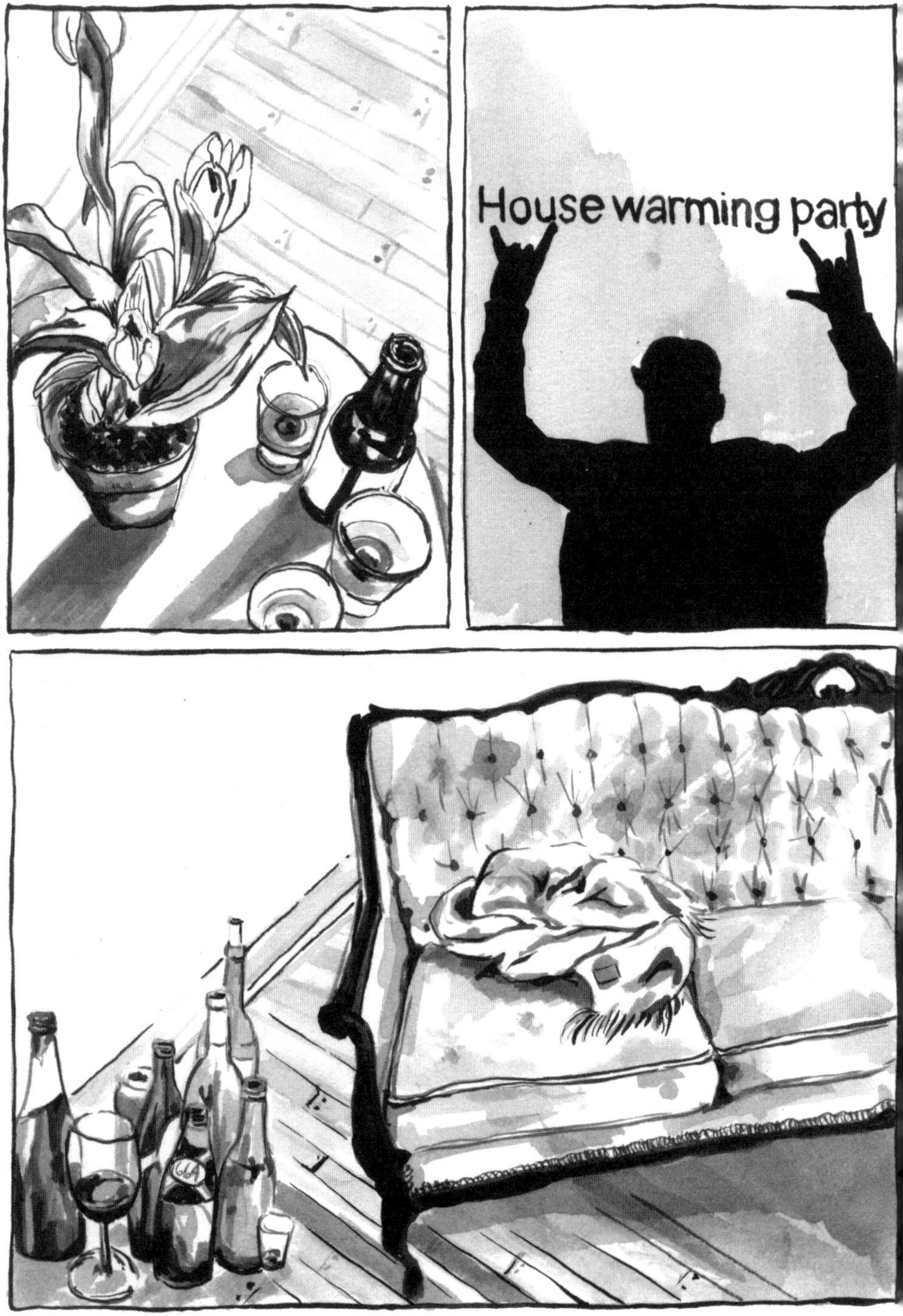
House warming party

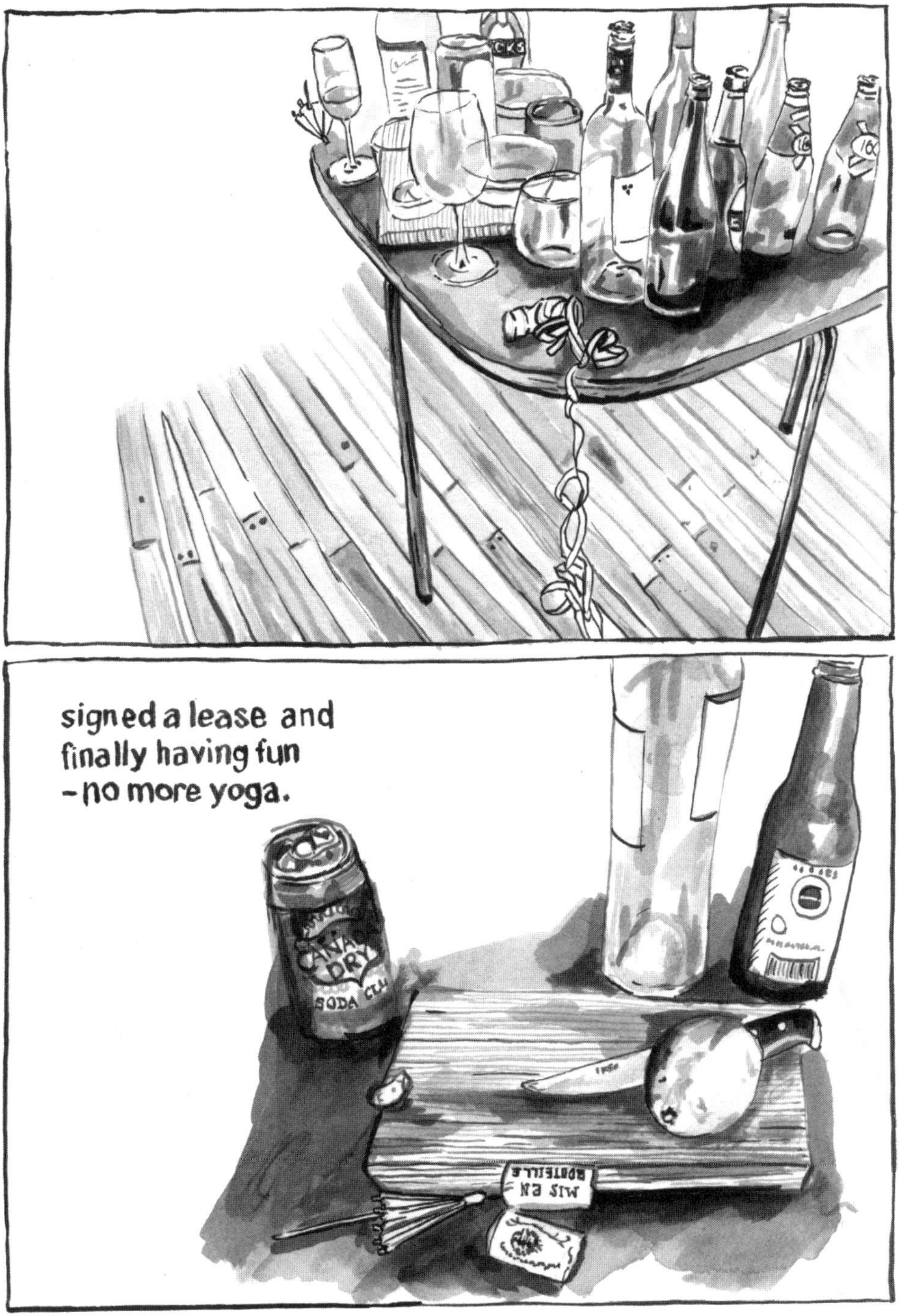
signed a lease and
finally having fun
-no more yoga.

the metro and Leonard Cohen forever

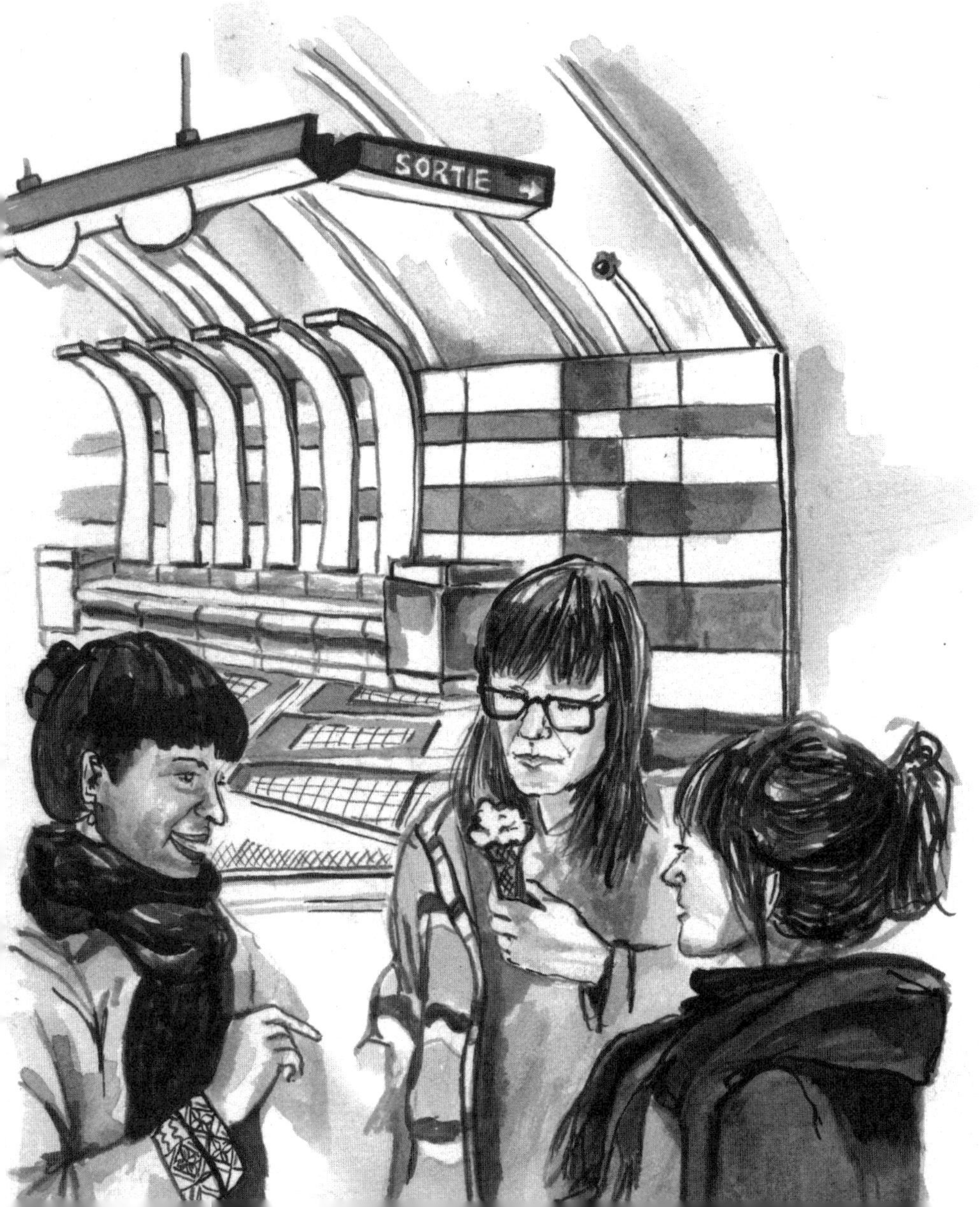
SORTIE

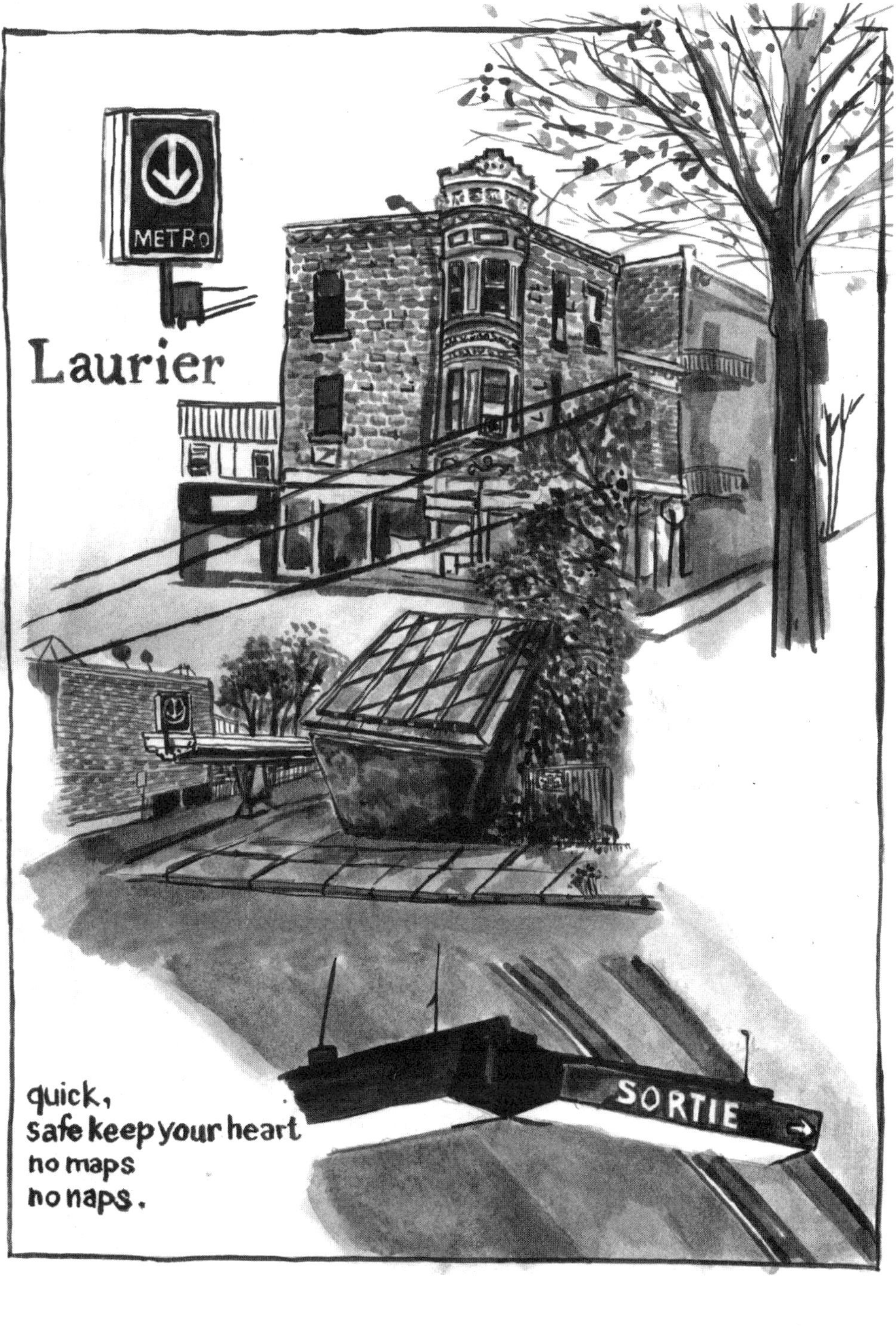
METRO
Laurier
quick,
safe keep your heart
no maps
no naps.
SORTIE

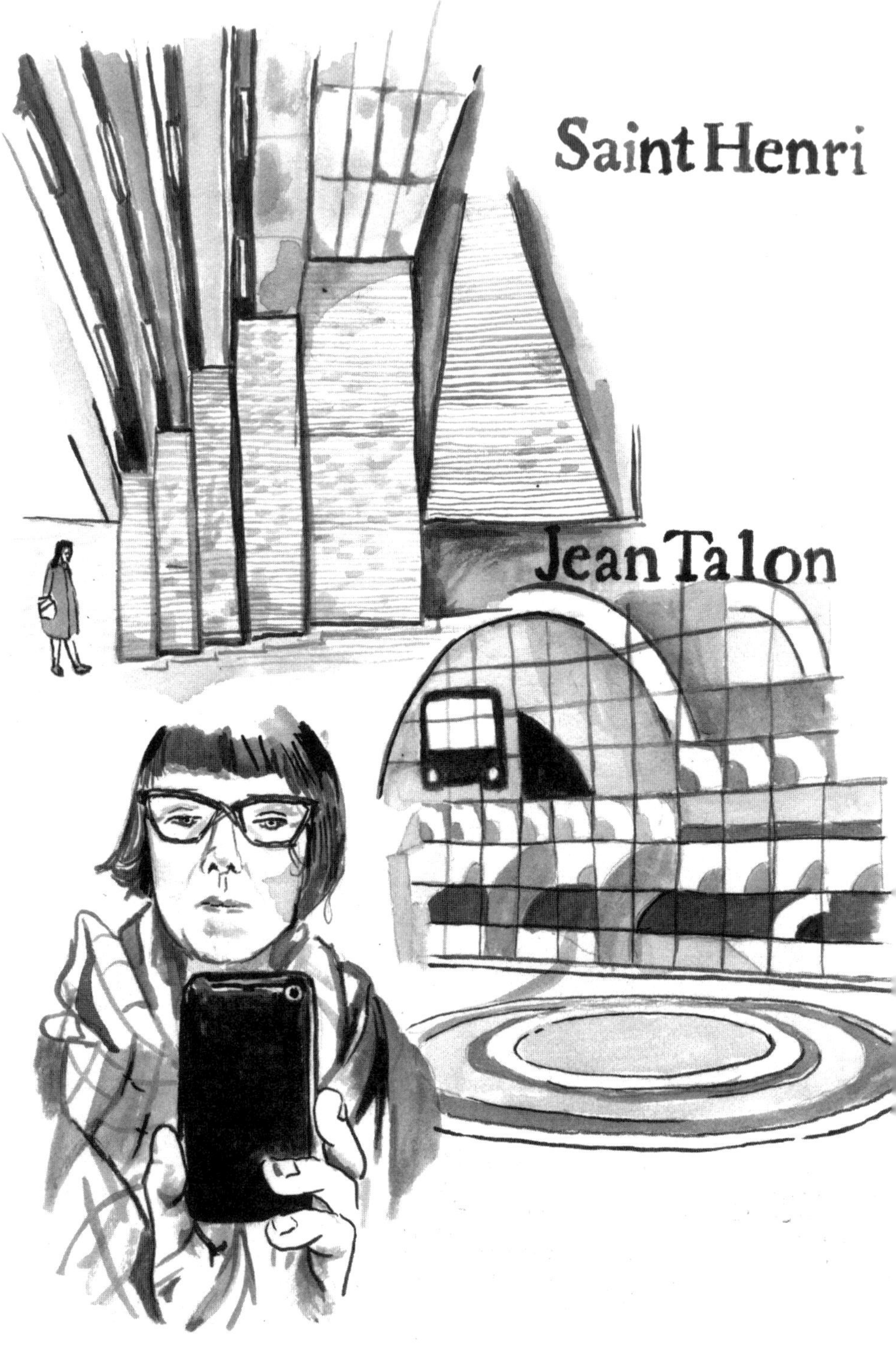
Saint Henri
Jean Talon

Berri UQAM

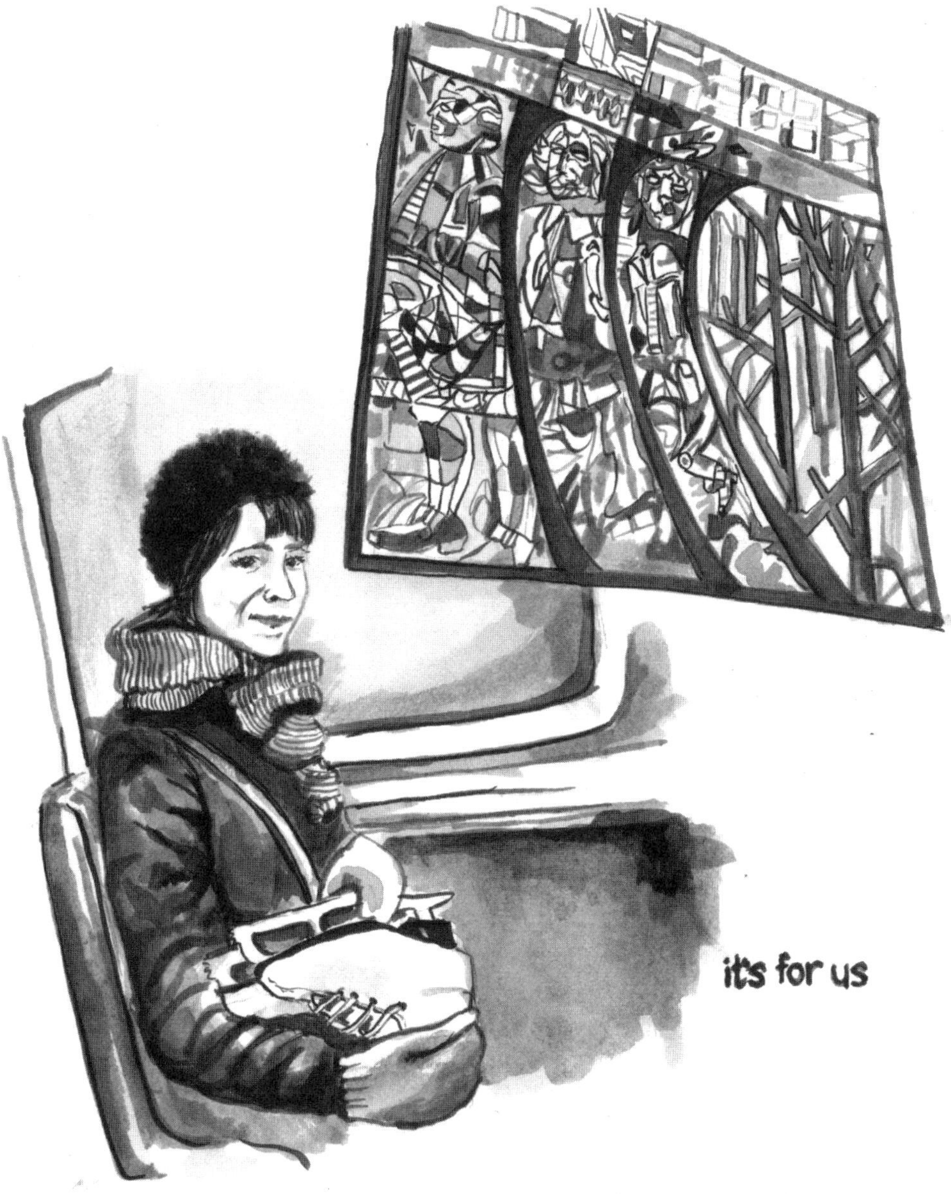
it's for us

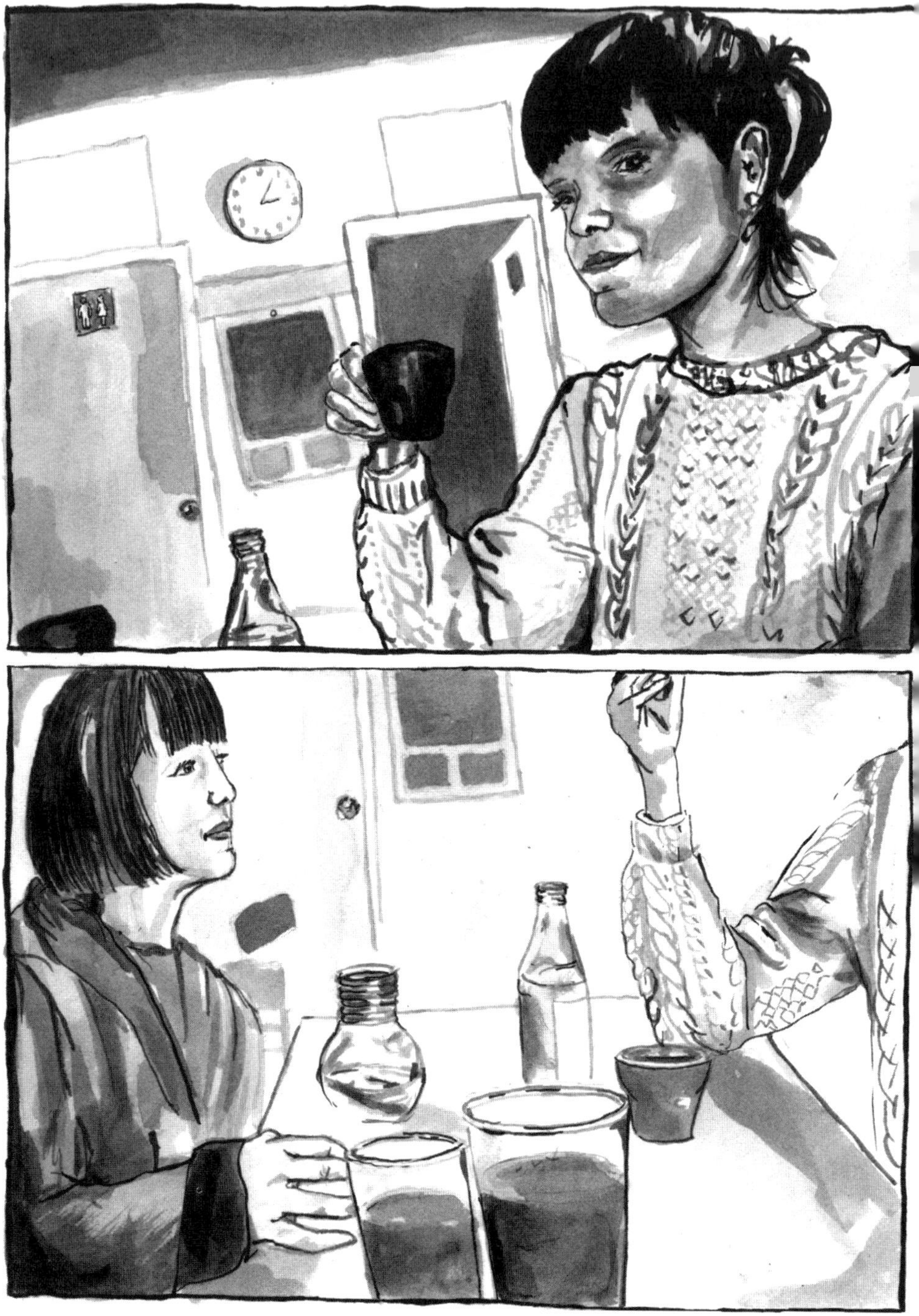

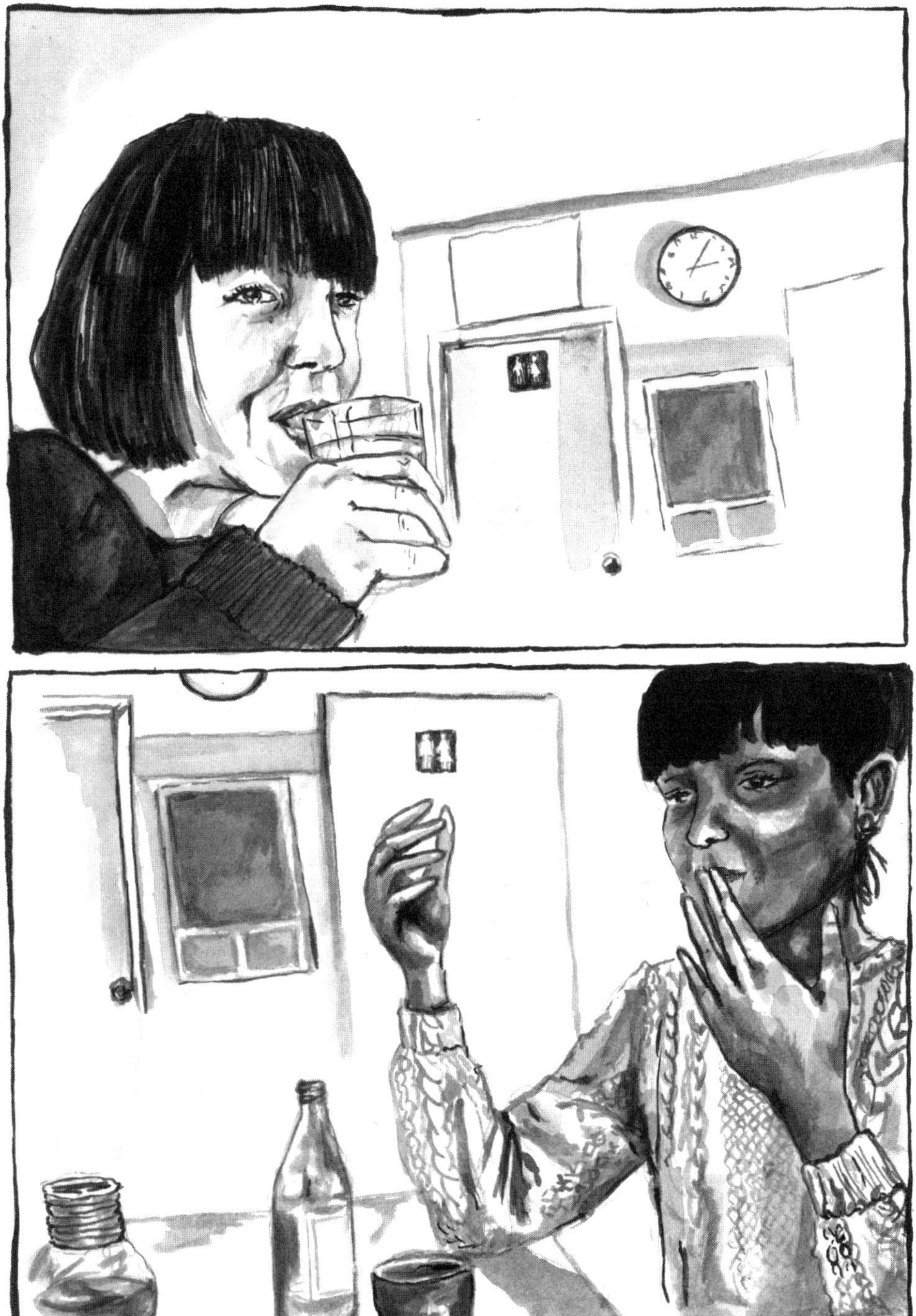

keep trying,
learn to fall

learn to jump
and land upright

do it again.

thank-you to:
meghan price
pavitra wickramasinghe
karin zuppiger
tim belliveau
laurenne belliveau
joanne porta
andy brown

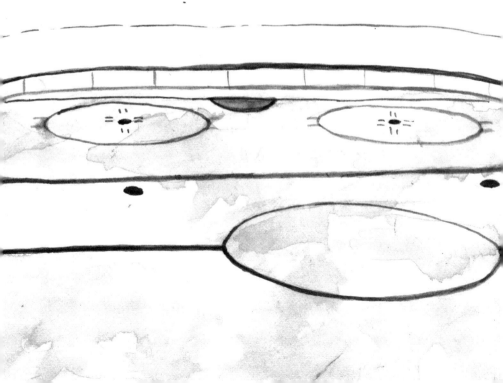